SEA FISHING FOR AMATEURS

SEA FISHING

FOR

AMATEURS

*A Practical Book on Fishing from Shore,
Rocks, or Piers*

WITH A DIRECTORY OF FISHING STATIONS ON THE
ENGLISH AND WELSH COASTS

By **FRANK HUDSON**

EIGHTH EDITION

ILLUSTRATED

PREFACE.

THE object of this book is to teach all who wish to learn, how to catch sea-fish, great and small. Within the limits of a small manual it is of course impossible to dilate at great length on any particular detail; but an endeavour has been made to include in these pages such practical information—based on years of experience—as will enable the merest novice to try his hand successfully at any of the various methods of fishing in vogue along our shores.

To those who go to the seaside for their annual holiday, it is expected that this little volume will be of special value, as it will not only enable them to select the place best calculated to give good results at the time of the year at which they are able to get away, but will also advise them as to the best way to set about fishing.

F. H.

CONTENTS.

Sea Fishing for Amateurs.

CHAPTER I.

INTRODUCTION.

IN hunting, shooting, racing, and angling, Englishmen are supreme. By English authors have been written the best guides to those sports; yet, strange to say, there is one branch of sport in which, as islanders, we ought to be leaders, but which is little thought of, as a rule. I refer to sea-coast fishing—one of the most healthful and delightful of pastimes. Indeed, I very much doubt whether there is any other description of sport so calculated to afford strength to brain, lung, and muscles. What can be more beneficial than a row over the dancing waves, each stroke of the oar expanding the chest, and each breath you take laden with life-giving ozone?

If any jaded, over-worked townsman would but follow my prescription for one fortnight in the summer season, I would guarantee to send him back to town strong as a lion and clear as a bell. To such a man I would say: Run down to some out-of-the-way fishing village with a good rocky coast. Take with you about 30 fathoms of brown sea-line, a couple of dozen looped hooks of various sizes, three leaden "sinkers," a few yards of whip-cord or "snooding," a sharp jack-knife, and a square, wooden frame. Purchase the line and snooding at a rope-shop, thereby

saving half the money which you would have to pay
at a fishing-tackle shop. You can also save money
by buying the hooks and sinkers at an ironmonger's.
With these materials you can make a good service-
able line for casual fishing.

In the next chapter full directions are given for
rigging up all descriptions of sea-lines: but if you
have not time for, or do not care for the trouble of,
rigging up your own line, you can purchase one complete with frame for about 5s., though it will have
the disadvantage of not being half so trustworthy as
one you could rig up for yourself. When ground-
fishing you will not require any artificial bait; but
for whiffing or railing be sure to purchase one or
two of the most useful kinds to carry with you. When
natural bait is not forthcoming, or difficult to procure, they are simply invaluable, and splendid sport
can be obtained with them. A full description of the
most killing patterns will be given in subsequent
chapters.

Now, I will say that you arrived last night at the
village you have selected. You have put up at the
little white-washed inn, where you have had a sound
night's sleep, thanks to the sea air, and have just
enjoyed a hearty breakfast. You arranged with one
of the fishermen to have a boat and box of bait in
readiness by half-past ten. If there are any fresh
herrings or pilchards to be had, be sure to secure four
or five; they are always a safe bait for conger and
ground-fish. If you have bought the hooks and lines
as directed, it is high time to set about putting them
together. Wind the brown line round the frame
until you come to about 16ft. from the end; cut 8ft.
off, and divide it into four pieces. On one end of each
piece make a stout "black knot," and slip the other
end through the loop of a hook, which the knot keeps
from slipping off. But a better way is shown in
Fig. 13. When each piece of line has its hook on,
fasten them to the end of your long line which hangs
from the frame, leaving 2ft. clear between each. Now

run a yard of the whipcord through a sinker, and
fasten it to the extreme end of your line, and you are
ready. This is the quickest mode of rigging up a
line, and for casual fishing is quite as good as the
most elaborate ones. The reason for using whipcord
with the sinker is very simple: should the sinker
become "stuck," as sinkers will, you lose it, but save
your hooks; for, by pulling hard, the whipcord breaks.

And now the fisherman arrives, and you follow him
to the little harbour, where the boat awaits you, bob-
bing up and down. In another moment you are
bounding over the dancing waves, a delicious breeze
keeping off the too warm acquaintance of the morning
sun. When about half-a-mile from the shore the
boatman drops the anchor and produces the box of
bait. Allow him to bait the hooks, as you are a
novice, but watch well the operation. There is nothing
like practical experience in such matters, though in
Chapter III. I have described fully the process of
finding and using all baits. But here let me say that
as each locality round our coast has at least one specimen of the finny tribe peculiar to itself, so each
locality has some one special kind of bait. Neverthe-
less, a mussel, a whelk, a piece of fresh crab or fresh
herring, are good in all localities. Your boatman will
not be slow in criticising your line. Mark well what
he says, and give him an ounce of tobacco for his
information, which is worth pounds of tobacco to you.

And now the four hooks are baited—one with a piece
of fresh herring, one with a piece of crab, one with
a mussel, and the last with sand- or mud-worms.
"Pay out" slowly until you "feel bottom," then let
the line rest between the first and second fingers of
your right hand—the most exquisitely sensitive of
all the digits. The tide is beginning to run high,
and fish must be well on the feed. You will not be
long idle. There you go! you feel something nibbling—do not move a joint of your finger until you
feel a "chuck," followed by a wriggle; then haul in
as fast as you like. Up it comes, a splashing, flashing

codling, over 4lb. in weight. He has taken the whelk. On with another; see that the remaining hooks are all right, and then down again. You have scarcely touched bottom ere you feel a sharp chuck, and the line is well-nigh pulled from your fingers. You pull in with all your might, the line swaying to and fro, for there is 5ft. of a conger pulling against you. Up he comes, looking a regular juvenile sea-serpent. Do not be frightened; get his head over the edge of the boat, and, with your knife, give him a deep nick on the back of his neck—he will not give you much further trouble. Get him into the boat, but take care that he is quite dead ere you attempt to remove the hook. Perhaps, as this is your first conger, you had better let your boatman do the business. Next to the ground-shark, the conger is the strongest and most voracious of all our coast-fish. He has taken the herring, so on with another piece, and lower again. You are kept busy with codling, rock-bream, flounder, pollack, and conger, and after a couple of hours you begin to feel awfully hungry, so your boatman raises the anchor and rows you home to luncheon.

Try this for one fortnight, my weary, jaded friend, and if I am not correct in my surmise as to the result, may I never catch and cook another blue-backed pol·lack!

CHAPTER II.

LINES AND TACKLE.

FOR general fishing—that is, when fishing for "anything and everything" that may take a fancy to your bait—I have in the previous chapter given a description of the tackle to use. In this chapter I propose to describe the various kinds of tackle required for different fish.

LINES, FRAMES, AND SINKERS.—When hand-line fishing (which is one of the most productive modes of sea-angling), I have always found "waterproofed" cod-line to be the most reliable. These lines are generally made of hemp, and are obtainable at any seaside tackle shop. Cotton lines are often used, but are not so strong as hemp; while those composed of flax are principally employed for the finer stuff where great strength is necessary. Four useful sizes for hand-lines are shown in Fig. 1. The largest is suitable for extra heavy work, such as congering; No. 2

No. 1.

No. 2.

No. 3.

No. 4.

Fig. 1.—Four Sizes of Lines most useful for Sea Fishing.

for deep-sea fishing; No. 3 for lighter leads and whiffing; No. 4 for chads, pout, dabs, and all smaller fish in-shore. They weigh respectively 21lb., 15lb., 9lb., and 6lb. per dozen 60yd. lines, which will be a guide in ordering, and this length will be sufficient for any style of fishing. Besides the main line, procure a couple of hanks of "snooding"—one very fine, and the other coarser.

The main line must now be stretched to prevent its "kinking," and the best place for this operation is in a field, or along a straight, unfrequented road. Attach

one end to a gate-post or other object, and, walking
backwards, carefully uncoil the line, holding it on the
two hands like a skein of wool. When unwound, proceed to the place of attachment, and having grasped
the line firmly with a piece of stout shoe-leather, walk
slowly along the entire length, straightening out the
" turns " as you go. On reaching the loose end, stretch
the line by pulling at it fairly hard. Repeat the above
process several times until the line has become pliable
and no more " kinks " are left in it, when you can con-
veniently fish with it. Lines are often " barked," or

Fig. 2.—Ash Frame for Lines, showing (A) cork bung for reception
of hooks.

tanned, in order to preserve them. Coil up the line
neatly, and, having placed it in a tub or bucket, pour
upon it a boiling solution of catechu and water ($\frac{1}{4}$lb. of
catechu to 3 pints of water). Leave it in the mixture
for twenty-four hours, then remove it, rinse in fresh
water, and hang it up to dry.

I always carry two main lines, one 60yds. and the
other 100yds. in length, mounted on good ash frames
(Fig. 2). Frames for deep-sea lines should measure
12in. by 9½in., and those for whiffing or railing
8½in. by 6in.; but the size, of course, varies according
to the length of the lines. A is a cork bung in which

to stick the hooks when winding, and preserve their points. All winders should be given two coats of

Figs. 3 and 4.—Oval and Conical Leads for Deep-sea or Paternoster
Fishing.

yacht-spar varnish to keep out the wet. After fishing, always dry your line carefully; and, when partially dry, re-wind it evenly upon the frame.

Fig. 5.—Pipe-lead for Horsehair or Whiffing Lines. The dotted lines show the hole passing through the centre for receiving same.

Make a large loop at the end of your line, either spliced or "whipped," from which hang your sinker, for reasons given in Introduction. The size of sinkers must vary according to the swiftness of the current.

Different sizes must be tried until the right one is
found. Figs. 3, 4, and 5 show the shapes of those I
have always found the best. They are always made
of lead, and can be obtained cheaply from any seaside
ironmonger's shop. For throw-out lines, a flat-sided
lead, either long or round, fitted with a brass ring, is
employed. The boat-shaped lead is another most
useful kind, having an eye of brass wire at each end.

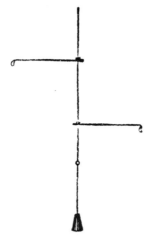

Fig. 6.—Portion of Line ready for Tackle, showing the two booms of
whalebone with loops at end for attaching the snoods.

Always bend on your lead with a loop, and avoid
knots, which are most troublesome to untie when wet.
    When the main line is ready, get four or five pieces
of round whalebone, about 1¼ft. in length and tapering at one end. Affix them to the end of your line,
about a yard apart, the bottom one being about 2ft.
from the loop (see Fig. 6). There are various methods
of fastening them on; but, as usual, the simplest way
I have found to be the most durable, and is as follows:
Make a notch, extending nearly round the whalebone,

about ½in. from the thick end, and then tie the line round it in a hard knot, which must be tightly bound with well-waxed housewife thread. Never mind the bulky appearance of the knot—the fish won't. Whip a copper-gimp loop, with waxed thread, to the tapering end of the whalebone (taking care to varnish well after), and the process is complete. You can affix any description of tackle to your line, and fish in any depth you like, by simply lengthening the sinker-cord. By the way, do not be sparing in the size of the loops.

Fig. 7.—**Deep-sea Rig with brass boom, lead, and gear complete.** The end of the main line is attached to the eye at the top.

For deep-sea fishing, Fig. 7 shows an excellent rig, an improvement upon that used in Guernsey. The boom is 11in. long, and made of ⅛in. brass wire. One end is formed into an eye, and the other bent into a spiral form, which revolves upon a brass reel. Through the centre of the reel runs a brass pin with an eye soldered on to the top and bottom. Attach the end of the line to the top ring, and the lead to the lower one by an independent piece of cord. Any ironmonger would make this boom to order. The snooding should be in one piece, 1½ fathoms long, and so arranged that one bait is nearer the bottom than the other. Sometimes there is a "sid" strap, about a fathom long, to which the snood is attached. Insert a swivel between the "sid" strap and snood, and always use those of brass or German silver for sea-fishing. The boat-shaped rig is easily fitted up, as there is no boom required, and the sheer of the lead keeps the snooding clear of the main line. In using the former, put the baits overboard, and let the snooding stream away with the tide, then lower the lead, and pay out as fast as you like. The boat-shaped lead, however, must be cast as far as possible from the boat after letting out the baits.

HOOKS AND TACKLE.—Always procure the best quality of hooks for sea-fishing, and make sure that they are British made. Inferior hooks of foreign manufacture are often offered. Several different sizes will be needed, but the following is a general guide: For bream, whiting, gurnards, and the usual ground-fish, use No. 3/0 round bend; mackerel, Nos. 1 or 1½ Limerick bend, and the same for pollack of average size. For large pollack, No. 6/0 is a useful size. Cod and conger require Nos. 7/0 to 10/0 round bent hooks. Besides the above, always carry a few sizes of "Pennell," Limerick, or Ball's eyed hooks for attaching to gut, the new numbers being hereafter quoted. For ordinary ground-fishing, use fine snooding; but in-shore, single or double gut. More particulars about tackle and what to use will be supplied later on. Always steep your gut tackle in fresh water for a few minutes after use; this preserves it. Loose hooks should be kept in a shallow box, having a tray with several compartments in it, to keep each size separate.

TYING GUT-COLLARS.—The best gut is round and white, and should be always kept in a dark place. Never buy the yellow stuff sometimes exhibited in shop windows. Before tying the gut, choose round strands, and cut off the "curly" ends, then steep in lukewarm water for a few minutes until soft. Take

two of the strands, and tie a single overhand knot
round the opposite strand. Reverse the ends, and do
the same on the other side (see Fig. 8). Draw each

*Fig. 8.—Single Fisherman's Knot, showing the ties quite loose before
tightening and drawing the two strands together.*

knot tight, and slide them together before cutting off
the ends. Fig. 9 shows a still stronger fastening, the
end in each case being passed twice through the loop.
Haul one knot fairly taut before making the other.

*Fig. 9.—Double Fisherman's Knot, the end in each case having been
passed twice round the opposite strand and through its own loop.*

These are the single and double fisherman's knots.
The loop at both ends of the cast or collar should be
formed as shown in Fig. 10. For attaching snooding
or fine line to a loop, Fig. 11 depicts a capital knot,

*Fig. 10.—Knot for Gut Loop, showing the two single knots before drawing
them together.*

easily undone. Make a stopper knot at the end before
forming the bend.

ATTACHING HOOKS.—The usual method of attaching
snooding to a hook with a "tang" is shown in Fig. 12,
but do not use it for gut. Make two "half hitches"

on the shank, then pass a third over the bend of the
hook, and haul taut. "Pennell" or eyed hooks are now
generally used for gut, and Fig. 13 shows a simple way
of attaching them, which I think will be quite clear.

Fig. 11.—Sheet Bend or Jam Knot, the end having been put through the
loop, brought round the two sides, and passed under its own part.

Of course, the simple bend (Fig. 11) can be adopted,
but it is sometimes apt to slip. Another secure plan
is to pass the end through the eye, bring it round the

Fig. 12.—Tying Snood to Hook, showing the third half-hitch passed over
the bend, the two former having been already pulled taut.

shank, return it through the eye, and then tie one half
of a double fisherman's knot (see Fig. 9) upon the
main strand. This is a good fastening for gut substitute. Gut is also whipped on to hooks with tapered

Fig. 13.—Double Jam Knot, the end of the gut being put through the eye,
passed twice around the shank, and inserted beneath both turns.

shanks. Take some strong red silk twist, well wax it,
and bind the gut evenly to the shank. Leave a loop
with the first end, take two or three turns over it,
then draw it "home" with the other end. Bite the

end of the gut slightly before attaching. **Fig. 14**
shows the process when nearly completed. Keep your
cobbler's wax in a cardboard pill-box, and moisten

Fig. 14.—Whipping Gut to Hook, showing mode of finishing, a loop having been left with the first end and the working part put through it.

your thumb before drawing the silk through. Whippings should be varnished with shellac varnish, made
by dissolving shellac in methylated spirits until it is
as thick as treacle. Apply with a small brush, and
keep the varnish tightly corked when not in use.

CHAPTER III.

SANDY-BOTTOM FISHING.

ADVICE as to the choice of fishing-grounds is very
difficult to give, and for this reason—those who go
sea-fishing generally do so for holiday pleasure.
Bachelors would probably prefer visiting some lively
quarter, where, after hauling in fish all day, they
could spend the evening in some " hall by the sea "
or other place of entertainment. Married people would
choose some quiet spot, with a flat beach and sands,
where the tide recedes for a mile or so, leaving a
splendid play-ground for the children to build sand-
castles on, as at Rhyl or Conway. Some will have
nothing but tall cliffs; and others, like myself, prefer

a low, rocky coast, which, by the way, is by far the best sort of place for fishing purposes. I will merely state here that the Cornish coast is the locality for big fish; while to those who wish to combine beauty of scenery with rocky and sandy grounds in close proximity (not to mention the convenient trains every half-hour to town and theatre), I would recommend a visit to Dalkey, on the Dublin coast. Ballycotton, in Cork, is a splendid place for varied sea fishing.

When you reach the place you have chosen, make a bargain with one of the boatmen for the hire of his

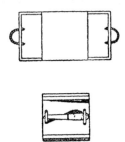

Fig. 15.—Top of Bait-box with Cover in Position, and showing knife
attached underneath the lid.

boat at so much per week; this you will find a far cheaper plan than hiring one by the day. Arrange with him also for the supply of bait, unless you wish to hunt for it yourself. Do not forget to find out what the chief local bait is. I find it advisable always to carry a few ringed hooks when "going out," in case of emergency; they can be quickly slipped on to any tackle, as described in the introductory chapter.

There are certain kinds of fish that haunt sandy grounds, such as the plaice, and there are others that prefer a rocky locality, such as the conger; then there are other fish found in all waters, such as cod, gurnards, mackerel, and bass.

BAITS.—Before setting out for a day's fishing it is most important to have a supply of first-class bait. and make sure that it is quite fresh—the fresher the bait, the better the sport. Order all the bait the day before, to be certain of getting it. Nearly all ground-fish will take pieces of fresh fish cut up, and of these pilchard is the most enticing, owing to its oily nature.

Fig. 16.—Shoemaker's knife, used for cutting baits.

When unprocurable, herring will make a fair substitute. Mackerel is also a capital bait, and a few can often be captured on the way to the ground (see Chapter VI.). Fig. 15 shows the bait-box complete and the inside of cover, with knife attached. It merely consists of a common box, 18in. by 9in., with removable cover upon which to cut up the fish. There

Fig. 17.—Method of Cutting Baits, the slanting lines indicating the Divisions.

is a handle at each end, formed with fine rope, for moving it about, or washing it overboard after fishing. The bait-knife, which is the common sort used by shoemakers, is shown more clearly in Fig. 16. First scale your fish, then insert the knife at the tail-end, and remove both sides close to the back-bone; throw the remainder overboard to attract the fish. Each side must be now cut up into diagonal strips about 1in. wide (Fig. 17). To bait the hook, pass the point

once through near the end, turn it over, and bring it
again through the same side (see Fig. 18). Longnose,
or gar-fish, is another excellent bait for conger, pollack, &c., and is caught on a small hook or triangle
when whiffing. Of all baits mussel is the most
generally used, and they are found clinging to rocks
and piers. Open mussels before you start, placing
them upon a piece of board. In opening them intro-
duce the knife at the broad part and pass the blade
completely round before attempting to separate the
two shells. Insert the hook through the leathery
tongue, pass it between the two halves, and finally
stick the point through the round gristle with
which the mussel holds its shell together. Rag or
mud-worms are excellent for rod-fishing from piers

Fig. 18.—Hook Baited, the point being passed through the fleshy
side twice.

or rocks. They are found in harbour mud chiefly, or
under stones amongst rocks. Keep them in a shallow
box, with the seams pitched, and containing a little
sea-water. Tilt the box slightly so that the worms
can crawl out of the water. An empty tobacco-tin
is also useful for carrying them to the scene of action.
Cuttle or squid are captured by tying a piece of fresh
fish to the end of a line, lowering it to the bottom,
and then drawing it slowly to the surface. When a
cuttle has seized it, coax him up gently, when your
companion must gaff him and hold him under water
until he has discharged the inky fluid. The cuttling
gaff consists of a long rod, with several square-bent
hooks lashed to one end, the barbs having previously
been filed off. Launce are dug out of the sand at
low-water spring tides, throwing the spadefuls quickly
on to the dry surface. When a launce is unearthed,

seize it quickly with the hands, and place it in a bucket or basket with some sand. Try close to the edge of the water. They are also captured with a launcing-hook (Fig. 19). This is passed through the sand at a depth of about 6in. until a fish is felt, when it is raised quickly and transferred to the basket. A moonlight night is the best for this amusement, when the tide is dead low, about 10 or 11 p.m. Sand-eels are also taken in numbers with a special ground-seine having fine meshes. Whelks and hermit crabs are obtained by trawling or dredging. Other good baits are soft crab, lug-worms, chads, and smelts.

Fig. 19.—Launcing Hook, consisting of a piece of hoop-iron bent at one end and fitted into a wooden handle.

TAKING MARKS.—In going out ground-fishing it is most important to have proper " marks," such as are shown in the charts in the last chapter. These should be ascertained from a reliable local man, and jotted down in a book for future guidance. Bring two conspicuous objects in the landscape, such as a flag-staff and a house, in a line with one another. Then turn the head one-quarter round, and get two other noticeable features of the land in conjunction. Anything that can be plainly seen and is permanent will answer the purpose. By this means you can always in clear weather return to the same spot again. It is better to always take marks " on the square "—*i.e.,* at an angle of 45 degrees. Never go out in foggy weather without a reliable boatman. When anchored, ground-baiting is most useful, and consists of placing pieces of offal or broken fish into a bag of fine netting and lowering it with a stone. Shake it up occasionally by pulling at the rope, and so attract the fish to the spot.

THE COD.—This fish shares with the herring the honour of being more sought after than any other denizen of the deep. From the banks of Newfoundland to Dublin Bay it is the object of pursuit to thousands of hardy fishers. The drying, salting, and curing of cod-fish in Newfoundland alone is a sight worth seeing; while a visit to Billingsgate any early morning during the season would give the reader some idea of its importance as a marketable commodity in London. Most wonderful things are to be found in the cod's stomach, and naturalists often purchase the entrails in order to examine their contents. In one instance a man's finger, with a gold ring upon it, was found to have been swallowed by a large cod. An extensive cod fishery is carried on in the North Sea. I have always found night the best time for catching this fish; but it will always bite freely in the daytime when the tide is rising. You must row out to proper "marks" in deep water, and use a heavy sinker. Bait with whelk, sand-launce (known as "hairy bait"), lugworms, or mussels. When using whelk, put the hook right through it, then sink the point deep in its toughest part. Hook the sand-launce, and all bait of that description, just as you would an earth-worm when fresh-water fishing, the only difference being that for large fish, like the cod, you run three or four launce on each hook. Use ordinary cod hooks with strong snoods, either attached as Fig. 12 or lashed on to the shank. The deep-sea rig (Fig. 7), or boat-shaped gear, is usually employed. Lower your lead until it touches the bottom, then haul up until your baits are just clear of the ground.

THE CODLING.—This lively young customer is to be caught in all localities where the water is of any depth. I have taken it at about thirty yards from the shore; it comes in with the tide, and will gobble whelk, mussel, crab, or sand-launce. When baiting with crab (hermit or soldier crab), always bind it to the hook with a couple of lashes of pink silk; this will prevent it washing off the hook by the action of the water. Use ordinary ground-lines or paternosters with finer snoods or gut, and round bent hooks, No. 3/0, or " Pennell " hooks, Nos. 2 or 3.

THE HERRING.—Someone has called the herring the " King of the Sea," and Thackeray wrote a glowing description of it in one of his papers. Scotch people call them the "lives of men." Certainly, the herring is the best-known, and, among the masses, the most popular, of all fish, in either river or sea. Even those people who have never been within fifty miles of the "briny" know the herring under its various disguises—kipper, " soldier," or bloater. It is not my mission here to enter into the divers theories anent this fish's habits, or to speculate on the probable locality it comes from, and eventually—if not caught —returns to. It is sufficient for fishermen to know that, at certain seasons, the herring visits our coasts in countless numbers, and is taken wholesale by netting. They do not often take bait; but I have caught them in both sandy and rocky localities, principally in the latter. Bait with small pieces of sand-launce or mud-worm. These fish are often taken on bare tinned hooks attached to light paternoster gear, and worked up and down with a sinking and drawing motion. They will also occasionally take a fly. At night they will take mussel or pieces of fish.

THE TURBOT.—This fish is particularly fond of sandy bottoms, like his cousins the sole and plaice. It is held to be a great table delicacy, and generally commands a good price in the market. Professional fishermen—I mean those who earn their bread by the business—generally use the trawl-net; but the amateur who uses the hand-line entices his lordship with the sand-launce, or a piece of smelt, letting the bait rest on the ground. Hook the smelt in the same manner as the whelk. Use round bent hooks, Nos. 3/0 or 4/0.

THE FLOUNDER.—This fish also is a lover of sandy bottoms, and is seldom met with in rocky grounds. It is fond of all kinds of soft baits, such as the sand-launce

and mud-worm, small pieces of which should be used.
Use "Pennell" hooks, Nos. 8 or 9, and let the
bait rest on the ground.

SOLE, PLAICE, BRILL, AND SKATE.—All these (the
first of which is considered a table delicacy, and commands its price) are fond of sandy bottoms and pieces
of soft bait. They bite greedily when the tide is
rising. Move the boat about a hundred yards nearer
to the shore every fifteen minutes. Let the bait rest
on the ground. The plaice is usually taken on "spil-
lers," and the brill in trammels and trawl-nets. It is
quite exceptional to take soles with a hook and line,
the demand for these fish being almost entirely supplied by net-fishermen. Use strong ground-lines and
hooks Nos. 6/0 to 10/0 for skate.

THE HADDOCK.—This fish, which, when salted and
cured, is such a favourite on the breakfast-table with
all sorts and conditions of people, like the herring, is
to be met with in almost every kind of locality; but,
unlike that silvery inhabitant of the sea, it is a great
feeder. It visits our coasts in enormous shoals, and
will take almost any kind of bait, such as pieces of
fresh herring, mussels, or whelks. Fish as for codling.

THE WHITING.—This delicious little fish is to be
found in all localities, but generally some distance
from the shore. It is usually caught in the daytime
on recognised whiting-grounds some way from the
coast. Use ordinary ground-line or paternoster, and
bait with fresh herring, or pilchard, or mussels. Fish
close to the bottom. Hooks Nos. 3/0, round or Kirby
bend, or "Pennell" hook, Nos. 5 or 6.

THE BASS, OR SEA-PERCH.—This fish is rather a
powerful customer to deal with, and when fishing for
it, it is well to always have the gaff in readiness. It
takes bait more freely in the early morning, and
generally musters strongly near the mouth of a river.
When bass are shoaling on the surface it is more difficult to catch them than at any other time. The best

baits are artificial spinners, sand-launce, live prawn, ray's liver, squid, pilchard, and soft crab (see " Rod-fishing "). Try at different depths. Hooks vary in size.

THE GREY MULLET.—This sporting fish is much sought after by the rod-fisher, so I will reserve my description for that chapter. It is fond of estuaries, and ascends the tidal parts of rivers, and may be seen wherever there are particles of decaying vegetable matter floating about upon which it feeds.

THE SMELT.—This little fellow is another frequenter of the mouths of rivers. It has a peculiar odour, which has been said to resemble cucumber. Smelts are fond of mud-worms and mussel. A full description of how to fish and the tackle to use will be given in Chapter V.

CHAPTER IV.

ROCKY-BOTTOM FISHING.

ROCKY ground is, as I have before stated, the best for fishing purposes—I mean an " iron-bound " bay or sound, in which there is water at all times, and in which you can fish at all periods of the day or night, though the best sport is to be obtained when the tide is rising. In such places, certain fish—the conger, for instance—remain constantly (there being always water), and grow to enormous proportions. Besides rock-haunting fish, other wanderers of the deep will also be met with—*e.g.*, the herring, cod, haddock, and others of that class. Moreover, if you are in search of health as well as sport, always select a rocky coast. I once heard an eminent member of the faculty say that the seaweed which grows on rocks emits an odour which is simply " life-giving." Yes; pitch your tent on rocky ground. So much for health; now for the fish.

THE CONGER.—This fish takes bait best in the night-
time, especially if the night is a very dark one. But
it will also give good sport by day, as the tide comes
in. Once the tide is at its height, conger cease to bite,
having probably eaten quite enough. By the way,
let me here remark that I have always found fish taken
at night to run much larger than those caught in the
day; this applies especially to the conger. It seems
that all large fish lurk in some hole, or under some
shelving rock, until darkness sets in. An "ancient
mariner" once told me that old, and consequently
big, fish "sleep all day." The conger is seldom found
away from rocks, and sometimes, when hooked, will
lash his tail round a convenient submerged boulder,
and defy all the fisherman's power to pull him from
his post. It is a remarkably strong and rather dangerous customer to tackle, and has been known to pull
a drowsy night-fisherman into the water by a sudden
jerk of the line. The conger will take almost any
description of bait, but the deadliest, especially at
night, is a strip of cuttle or squid, with a piece of
pilchard to give it a flavour. The bait for conger
should be as fresh as possible. The conger is a deadly
enemy of the cuttle-fish, which it boldly attacks and
tears to pieces. Special hooks (as shown in Fig. 19A)
should be used.

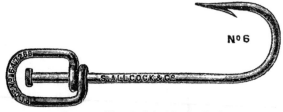

Fig. 19A.—Allcock's Swivel Conger Hook.

Be sure to have a large swivel on the line. Conger hooks,
when not required, should be well greased and wrapped in
an old worsted stocking. Allow a conger plenty of time

to take the bait, and do not strike until you feel the drag
of the fish making off with it. Before unhooking, cut the
conger at the back of the neck with a sharp knife, severing
the vertebræ. A heavy wooden club, or "priest," is
sometimes carried for killing a large specimen. Let your
bait rest on the ground, with the lead just raised from the
bottom. Always gaff conger towards the tail, if possible.
Large congers are also taken from piers and rocks in the
evening or after dusk by throwing out lines baited with
squid. A short stiff rod and a stoutly built reel, such as
the "Allcock-Bell," are essential.

THE POLLACK.—Of all sea-fish, the pollack affords
perhaps the best sport to anglers all round our coasts.
It is plentiful on the Irish coast, and in Scotland goes
by the name of "lythe." The ordinary pollack is

Fig. 20.—Putting on Lead Wire, showing process nearly completed.

olive-brown on the back, and lighter underneath, but
they vary a good deal in colour. When fresh, it is
excellent for the table; but it will not keep long, and
therefore is rarely exhibited for sale in large centres
of population. The "rauning" pollack, or coal-fish
(termed "saithe" in Scotland) is a distinct species, and
can be recognised by its leaden colour and a white stripe
down its side. Small coal-fish are called "billet" in the
North.

WHIFFING FOR POLLACK.—This is delightful sport,
and, when large fish of 8lb. to 10lb. in weight are plentiful, is very exciting. Use a hemp line, No. 3 size (see
Fig. 1), and, having stretched it, weight it by wrap-
ping lead wire around it. The lead wire should be cut
up into pieces, 10in. in length, and coiled evenly upon
the line with the fingers at one fathom's distance apart

(see Fig. 20). The last two or three fathoms, which
will be inboard, need not be weighted. Horsehair
lines, 22 fathoms long, and having a pipe lead at every
2 fathoms (see Fig. 5), are also excellent. The lengths
should be laid up in opposite directions, and two
different ones joined together, to prevent kinking.
Now attach a No. 2 German silver swivel to end of

Fig. 21.—End of Main Line, with swivel attached to spliced eye and top
portion of snooding.

line, and then 4 or 5 fathoms of fine snooding. The
best snooding is made of three strands of No. 18 Irish
flax netting-thread, for which apply to Messrs. Wm.
Good and Son, Ltd., 46, Fish Street Hill, Monument,
London, E.C. 3.   Fig. 21 shows end of main line, with
swivel and snooding attached.   At the end of the fine
stuff attach a German silver spring link (see Fig. 22), which

Fig. 22.—Spring Link, fastened to snooding by putting end through eye
and tying one-half of double fisherman's knot upon main part.

facilitates the removal of the gut-collar. Use a single,
double, or treble gut cast, 1yd. in length, according to the
run of the fish.
Artificial baits are now universally in request for
whiffing, and of these the red or black rubber eel is one
of the best. I prefer those with a spinner, but they are
often used without.   The "Lizard" sand-eel or "Chal-
lenger" bait is very killing.   Another excellent lure is
the ray's skin bait (Fig. 23), which may be tied on
a No. 6/0 or a No. 3/0 ringed Limerick hook, according to the size of the fish expected.   Having whipped
on the hook (see Fig. 14), take a piece of ray's skin

cut as per pattern, and, having folded it in half, lash
it to the top of the shank by two or three turns of
waxed silk. Take care that the rough, or flesh, side
is outermost. A tag of the same skin on the point of
the hook completes the bait. The spinner revolves
upon a brass pin, having an eye at both ends, which
is afterwards soldered. Obtain the white under-skin
of a large thornback, or ray, from a net fisherman,
and, having laid it upon a board, scrape off all the
remaining flesh with a blunt knife; then leave it in

Fig. 23.—Ray's Skin Bait, showing the lure complete and pattern for
cutting skin.

a sunny place till quite dry, when it becomes like
horn, but when wetted resembles a piece of white kid
glove. Instead of the tag of skin, you may bait your
hook with a piece of fresh longnose or mackerel, cut
from the tail part.

The Baby spinner resembles the bait above described,
but the hook should be No. 1½, and should revolve
upon either single or double gut whipped on to the
hook. A small "sneed," or slip of mackerel, usually
takes the place of a ray's skin. Use this bait for
mackerel and smaller pollack. Flies are sometimes
killing when fastened to the cast. The best of these is a
black or a red one, ribbed with silver tinsel, and having a

c

white wing. The eel-tail bait (Fig. 24) is a capital
lure for big pollack, and should be rigged upon a
large cod-hook. Catch a small fresh-water eel, and
cut off the head. Draw the skin down for an inch or
so, and sever the skinned portion. Pass the hook
through the body, bringing it out at the belly, and
draw the loose skin down so as to form a kind of white
head to the bait. Keep your eel-tails, when not required, in strong salt and water. You can fish with
this bait in deep water, up to 18 fathoms, where a
spinning bait could not properly be worked. Before

Fig. 24.—Eel-tail Bait rigged up complete on round-bent hook.

rigging up the eel, it is better to scour it with sand and
water to give it a whitish appearance. Lamperns, found in
rivers, are also good. Other baits, such as pork-rind or
gurnard-skin, are used in connection with spinners. One
or two large rag-worms, hooked on by the head, are most
enticing.
    In whiffing all the line, about 30 fathoms, is let out,
and the baits are towed slowly from the stern of a
rowing-boat. In-shore, 4 or 5 fathoms of line will be
sufficient, weighted with a small pipe lead; this will,
however, depend upon the depth of water. From 6 to
10 fathoms will be the most suitable depth in which
to fish. When using two lines, bait one with the

rubber eel and the other with the ray's skin, and weight one line more heavily than the other. Over rocky ground is the best locality, and engage a reliable man, a crabber for preference, who knows the ground. The best time to fish is the last of the ebb and the first of the flood. Always carry a strong gaff, and never go to sea without an extra line in the boat. Having let out your line, make the end fast around the thwart in case you should have to drop it to attend to the other line. If you should hook a heavy pollack, do not hold on too tightly, and if the fish requires line, allow it to slip through your fingers until he is exhausted. Gaff a fish, if possible, in the shoulder, and not in the head or tail. Try to keep a pollack from getting into the weeds, in which case he is almost certain to break away. The boat should be pulled faster for mackerel than for bass and pollack. If you are whiffing unaided by a man, make a loop in the line, and hold it on the forefinger of your right hand; you can thus pull and fish at the same time.

When whiffing, keep a sharp look-out for crab-pot " marks," as they may often, if hooked, occasion the loss of your gear. Wherever you see the corks, you may be sure you are on good fishing-ground.

As soon as the tide has become too strong for whiffing, anchor the boat and fish with a drift-line, using sand-eels or pilchard bait; but more about this under " Rod-fishing."

THE BREAM.—This is a handsome fish, to be met with on all parts of our coast where there are sunken rocks. My personal experience teaches me that the favourite feeding-ground of this species is the extreme end of some sunken ridge; there they multiply and grow fat. The evening is by far the best time for tackling them. If you are lucky enough to drop your line among them, you will be kept busy hauling them in between sundown and darkness. They are strong fish, but are easily landed, no matter what size. Bait with a small piece of pilchard, fresh herring, or mussel; they will also take sand-launce

or mud-worm. Employ ordinary ground-lines or paternosters, and fish just clear of the bottom.

THE HAKE.—Fishermen sometimes call this fish the
"female cod," and the flesh is excellent when fried or
baked. It is a savage fish, and works havoc amongst
herrings, and other fish of that class. Its appetite is in-
satiable, and it is ever on the watch for food. Shoals of
hake follow the herring and mackerel to our shores, and
frequently cut the herring-nets to pieces in their fierce
rushes after their prey. Yet, with all their feeding,
they never seem plump like the cod. Bait with pilchard
or herring, using strong snoods and hooks Nos. 6/0 or
7/0. Care must be taken when unhooking the fish, as
their jaws are very strong and sharp. Hake are
usually captured at night by pilchard or herring boats
at anchor. Try at different depths for this fish.

THE WRASSE.—This pretty specimen of the finny
tribe is generally to be met with where there are
plenty of sunken rocks, and especially near piers. It
is not of much value as an article of food, being rather
watery and soft. When the tide is just beginning to
rise, drop your line, baited with rag-worm or crab,
right down to the rocks, and you will have plenty of
sport. Use small "Pennell" hooks.

THE GURNARD.—This fish is another haunter of rocky
places or sandy bays, and lives almost entirely on
small crabs, whelks, and food of that class. It is
found all round our coasts, and in Ireland, where it
is very plentiful, is called the "gurnet." When lifted
into the boat it often emits a kind of grunt. The gurnard is one of those fish which require peculiar cook-
ing, being of a dry nature; indeed, there are few
people who know how to cook it properly. When
fishing for gurnard, bait with a piece of mackerel, crab,
or whelk. They can be taken with ordinary ground-
lines, or by whiffing slowly over a sandy bay, allowing
the baits to drag along near the bottom. The red and
grey are the commonest varieties, and the larger ones
are called "tubs."

THE MACKEREL.—This pretty and delicious little fish is a universal favourite with all classes, and during the season millions are sold in London alone. Its only fault is that it is a bad "keeper," often becoming tainted (and sometimes even dangerous as food) in a few hours. Few fish swimming in the sea afford such delightful sport, and there are several modes of catching them, either at anchor, or by whiffing and railing under sail, all of which have their champions. For myself, I prefer railing, or "reeling," to all the other modes, but have left that subject for Chapter VI. When fishing with a hand-line, use sand-launce or a narrow strip of mackerel. Employ fine groundtackle, and fish near the bottom. Very fine mackerel are often taken by drift-lining.

CHAPTER V.

ROD-FISHING.

OF all styles of sea-fishing this undoubtedly holds the pre-eminence as the most sportsmanlike method, and is becoming more popular every year. The advantage of a rod over the hand-line lies in the fact that finer lines can be used, and its elasticity enables the angler to play a large fish with greater certainty of ultimately landing him. From piers and rocks a rod will also afford capital sport to those unaccustomed to venturing in boats, and at most seaside places this delightful pastime may be indulged in.

RODS.—For general fishing a built cane rod of 7 to 8ft. is usual. To obtain satisfaction, purchase one made by a reputable manufacturer, such as Allcock's, Farlow's, or Peeks. The "Minchin" sea-rod—sold by Messrs. A. Carter and Co., 11, South Molton Street, Bond Street, London, W. —is recommended. It is double cane-built, and the length is 11½ft. for whiffing, spinning, etc.: or 7½ft. for bottom-

fishing. Another favourite weapon for heavy fish is the
" Ballycotton " rod, by the same makers, also double
cane-built with steel centre. The " B.S.A." is an excellent
pattern, and the length can be varied from 11ft. to 7ft.
6in., the latter short enough for boat-work. It is made
by Messrs. C. Farlow and Co., 11, Panton Street, London,
S.W. 1. For bottom-fishing or casting from the reel,
the pulley (Fig. 25) is useful in lessening friction, and can
be fitted to any rod-top with bicycle cement, the parts

Fig. 25.—Pulley with Line-Guard attached to top of " B.S.A." Rod.

having been previously warmed. I would recommend most
rods to be fitted with protected porcelain or agate rings to
ensure a free-running line. Greenheart is quite suitable
instead of split-cane, and rather less expensive. For
rock-fishing a rod of 12ft. to 16ft., the lower joints bamboo
and the tops greenheart, will be suitable. But for casting
baits a long distance, a rod of 7ft. to 9ft. is preferable. Old
salmon or trout fly-rods, also pike spinning-rods, will often
be very useful.

REELS.—For bottom-fishing, a 6in. reel of Nottingham pattern, with brass flange and optional check, will be required; or a 5in. size for bass and pollack. For pier fishing a 4in. is the best general size. Casting-reels should be of Nottingham style, with front and back plates of bakelite, or with brass flange. The " Aerial " is a good pattern. Nowadays non-corroding metal reels, such as the " Allcock Bell," and bakelite reels, such as the " Aerialite," are largely replacing wooden reels.

LINES.—Moderately fine hemp or flax lines are best, and, for heavy fish, 200yds. should be provided, but usually 100yds. is enough. The "Cuttyhunk" (Gamage's) and Carter's special sea line are excellent cable-laid Irish flax lines. Plaited lines are very good, as they avoid snarling. For pier angling 50yds. will be enough. Avoid silk or oil-dressed lines, which often rot. Always unwind lines and leave to dry, or use a line-drier.

GUT SUBSTITUTE.—This twisted silk fibre, resembling catgut, is now largely used. It is very cheap, durable, and a trace of any length can be used without knots. Perhaps the best kinds are "Ja-gut," sold by Messrs. S. Allcock and Co., Redditch; "Olympic" fibre (Messrs. A. W. Gamage and Co.). It is supplied in natural colour, dyed sea-green, or blue. The 40yd. coils are most economical, and the most useful sizes are Nos. 7 to 14. Fine salmon gut is useful for pier-angling, and should be wrapped up when not in use. For knots see Figs. 8, 9, 10, but avoid joining the substitute. Soak the substitute or gut in warm water before knotting. The figure-of-eight knot is reliable in connecting substitute to reel-line or the eye of a hook. Fine wire traces, fitted with swivels, are useful for heavy fish. Rinse traces in fresh water after use, dry carefully, and apply vaseline to wire tackle.

PATERNOSTERS.—For bottom-fishing prepare a strong cast of substitute or gut, about 2yds. long, with a loop at both ends, and to the lower one attach a small conical or pear-shaped lead. Now connect three " Pennell " or

" Ball's " eyed hooks to short pieces of gut provided with
loops, and affix to the cast at convenient knots by opening
loop and passing the hook through.   One-half of the loop
should be above the knot, and one-half below.   The lowest
hook-link should be close to the lead, and the others
18in. apart.   Use strong substitute or double gut for the
main line, and lighter for the hooks, according to class of
fish.   Fig. 26 shows how a swivel can be introduced;
slightly flatten the brass eye before attaching the hook-
link.   Leads must be changed according to the strength of

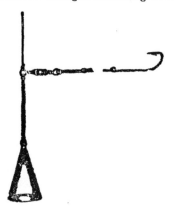

Fig. 26.--Lower part of Paternoster, showing lead and swivel inserted in
        cast, the hook-link being attached by a loop.

tide, but will rarely exceed ½lb. for inshore-fishing.   The
" Diamond Straight Pull " paternoster, made by Messrs.
Carter in different strengths, is an excellent pattern, but
there are many others.   Avoid as much as possible all com-
plicated tackle.   When angling for dabs and flat-fish, use
a longer trace for the lowest hook, and allow the bait to
rest on the bottom.   Dabs inhabit sandy or muddy bays,
and the best baits are mussels, lugs, or rag-worms.   The
dab closely resembles the flounder, but its under-side is
transparent white, instead of being opaque.

PATERNOSTER FOR PIER-FISHING.—Take a 1oz. pipe-lead
(Fig. 5), and having doubled and twisted a piece of copper
wire, 6in. or 7in. long, pass the ends through it. Leave a
loop projecting from the top, and secure the two lower
ends by inserting them through a small piece of flat lead,
turning the points back. Affix your cast to the upper loop,
and use two "Pennell" or "Ball's" eyed hooks, Nos. 5
to 11, the lower 6in. above the sinker, and the other 18in.
higher up. Bait with rag-worms, mussel, peeled shrimp,
or lugs.

Fig. 27 shows the rubber eel with spinner, exten-
sively used in whiffing from a boat for pollack and

Fig. 27.—Rubber Eel with Spinner on Cranked Hook, the upper eye of
the swivel being used for attaching the loop of the gut-cast.

bass, about which some directions have already been
given. Different colours are employed, but the best
is made of red rubber, though some prefer black.
White or grey rubber eels are very deadly for bass-
fishing. Always carry a pair of pliers with you to
repair a spinner in case it should become damaged.
Artificial eels should be rigged on No. 6/0 Limerick
hooks for large pollack, and No. 3/0 for smaller fish.
Plain eels, without a spinner, are in favour with many
anglers, but I always prefer the former, having made
large catches with it. The hook should be bent, or
cranked, so that the eel will revolve when drawn
through the water. Use a gut cast as already directed
in Chapter IV., and a small pipe-lead upon the reel-
line. Fig. 28 illustrates an improved lead, which

from its shape will always keep clear. When whiffing
for large pollack, use a short, stiff rod with double or
treble gut cast, and be very careful not to let the fish
take the bait to the bottom. Some use wire or phosphor
bronze traces, but, although strong at first, they are apt to
deteriorate quickly. A large landing-net should be
carried in the boat, as well as a gaff. In unhooking
a large fish, make a semi-circular cut under the
lower jaw, through which the hand may be inserted, and the bait loosened; then draw it out through
the mouth. Of course, this only need be done when
the fish has gorged the bait.

Fig. 28.—Geen's Patent Lead for weighting rod-line, with spring-hook
swivel on each side.

A good plan for catching bass when noticed near the
surface is to use a long salmon-rod, and a red eel without a spinner. Let out as much line as possible, and
keep the bait playing with the motion of the top joint.
" Feathero " artificial minnows are also excellent bait.
When whiffing has become impracticable, anchor
the boat, and fish with a drift-line, either using a
hand-line or a rod, or both combined. Large mackerel,
bass, and many other fish may thus be captured. Live
sand-eels are the favourite bait, and they should be
kept alive in a special basket, called a " courge," which
is towed to the fishing-ground. Rubber eels and spinning baits, or a piece of fresh pilchard or herring, are
also most enticing. Fig. 29 illustrates the method of
baiting a live sand-eel. Pass the hook—No. 2/0 or 3/0,
round bent—through the mouth, bring it out through
the gills, and catch the point through the skin of the
throat. A live sand-eel, hooked through the back skin with
a small triangle, is a deadly bait for bass. When ground-
fishing, always put a drift-line overboard, as you may
capture a shark, or other large fish.

Spinning with a rubber eel is excellent when fishing for bass from rocks—a favourite pastime with thousands of sea anglers. It is not much use trying, however, unless the surf is breaking upon the rock, or the water is discoloured. This dangerous, but fascinating, method may be practised from any steep rock having deep water alongside. Cast your bait out some distance, allowing it to sink; then draw it by a series of

Fig. 29.—Launce Baited. The hook is passed through the mouth, brought out at the gills, and lightly secured in the skin at the throat.

jerks towards the base of the rock. A dead sand-eel is also good, worked in the same manner, and pollack also show a great fondness for this lure. A whole side of a pilchard or herring is another capital bait for a bass, and Fig. 30 shows how to place it upon the hook. Crab-bait is frequently used in Cornwall for bass-fishing, and the fishermen there employ a large cod-hook, attached to strong whip-cord. When a fish

Fig. 30.—Pilchard Bait. The hook is inserted at the tail-end and again passed through it higher up.

seizes the bait he is heaved out unceremoniously, and landed upon the rocks. On a sandy beach grand sport may sometimes be enjoyed by wading in as far as possible and casting in your bait (a dead sand-eel), allowing it to rest upon the bottom. Then retreat on to the shore and wait until a fish carries off the bait, when you must strike and play him as well as you are able with the rod. One or two artificial flies are often

useful for bass and pollack, and sometimes sea-trout
are taken with a salmon-fly casting it from a rock near
the mouths of rivers. When angling from steep rocks
it is always advisable to carry a long-handled gaff with
you, and it is better to have a companion to come to
your assistance. I find a large fishing-basket the best
as a receptacle for fish, placing two or three sheets of
old newspaper at the bottom to keep it clean. Or, it
may have a lining of hessian, or thin canvas, removable for washing.

Pollacking from piers and rocks is a capital amusement, but requires some knowledge and skill. Use a

Fig. 31.—" Fishing Gazette " Float. The Peg is removed before inserting
the line through the slit.

fine reel line, to the end of which attach a single gut
cast of about 1 yard in length. A " Pennell " Limerick
hook, size No. 5, is the best, and it should be fastened to
the lower end of the gut as shown in Fig. 13. Weight the
gut with two or three small shot, or lead wire, but when
there is no current you may use a light line. The "Fold-
over" lead, made by Messrs. Allcock and Co., Redditch,
is a handy pattern, which is merely folded on the line, thus
dispensing with shot. Bait your hook with rag-worms so
as to leave two or three tails hanging down, and the livelier

your worms are the better. Separate any pieces from
the main stock of worms and keep them in another tin.
These portions will do very well for pout, chads, smelts,
&c., but pollack much prefer live bait. A float is often
desirable, and Fig. 31 shows an excellent kind, known
as the "Fishing Gazette" float. There is a slit in the
side through which to pass the line before pegging it.
In angling from rocks, allow the current to carry your
float some distance out to sea; you will thus stand
a better chance of hooking a good fish. The length
of line below the float will depend upon circum-
stances and the depth of water. Try different depths
for pollack. Always have sufficient lead on your line
to keep the float submerged as far as the light-coloured
portion, and upright in the water.

Fig. 32.—Grey Mullet Tackle, consisting of 1yd. gut cast, and taper quill
float, and weighted with four split shot about 1ft. above the hook.

Grey mullet occasionally afford grand sport to the
angler, though it must be confessed they are extremely difficult to capture. The best baits for mullet
are rag-worms or paste, but they will also take earth-

worms, pilchard, raw shrimp, or boiled macaroni. I
have illustrated the best tackle in Fig. 32, and a
No. 8 "Pennell" hook should be used. Light paternoster gear is also useful from piers and rocks. To
induce these fish to congregate in one spot, ground-
baiting is important. It should consist of pilchard or
refuse pounded up and thrown in occasionally. Or it
may be placed in fine netting or canvas and cast out
where you propose fishing. In brackish lakes this is
a capital plan. In the Channel Isles they use a kind
of shrimp ground-bait, called "chervin," a small
quantity of which is thrown in from time to time.
Allow a mullet plenty of time to take the bait, and do
not strike until the float has completely disappeared.
Play your fish boldly, and get him into the landing-
net as quickly as possible. Mullet should not be
handled rashly as their fins are very sharp, and they
should be knocked on the head before unhooking. Near
the mouths of rivers, or in estuaries, are good localities
to try. They often assemble near docks, and are seen
nibbling the green weed from the bottoms of ships. At
Plymouth docks these fish are regularly captured by the
pier anglers, baiting with rag-worm. Brandlings are a
capital bait for large mullet in brackish water, and you
may use a good-sized hook.

The best tackle for smelts is a fine gut paternoster, with
three or four small roach-hooks attached at intervals, baited
with small bits of rag-worm or peeled shrimp. Lower
the baits until near the bottom, when raise slowly to
the surface. The fish will follow the baits, and
become hooked. Two or more of these lively fish may
often be captured at a time, and the sport is decidedly
amusing. They will also take mussel or soft crab. A
single hook can, of course, be used if preferred, sinking
it with one or two small shot. The atherine, or sand-
smelt, is the species which frequents piers, the true
smelt being taken in rivers.

For all pier- and rock-fishing the flood-tide, during
the springs, is by far the most profitable.

CHAPTER VI.

MACKEREL-RAILING.

ONE of the pleasantest modes of sea-coast fishing, and a great favourite with the fair sex, is mackerel-railing, or "plummeting." It can be followed in nearly all waters round our coast during summer weather, and the reason why ladies choose it before all other styles of fishing is that there is no "nasty bait-hooking" required. Being always carried on under sail, a pleasant cruise can be combined with fishing, provided there is a certain amount of wind to drive the yacht along.

Fig. 33.—Rig for Plummeting, showing lead attached to loop, short boom resting upon knot, and portion of snooding.

LINE AND TACKLE.—The best sport is obtained with a stiffish fly rod, a light line, and not too much lead; but any ordinary hand-line can be used, and it need not measure more then 10 fathoms in length. Make a large loop at the end, with which to attach the lead. This should be of the conical pattern, weighing about 2lb., as it stands steadily upon the deck when hauled in, and will not roll about like circular ones. Boat-shaped or round leads, with a brass eye at each end, are popular kinds, but the former are apt to sheer about, and do not travel steadily through the water.

Fig. 33 illustrates the best rig for plummeting. The boom is formed out of the handle of an old toothbrush, by cutting off the brush part, and rounding it nicely with a file. A hole is then bored at each end, one being larger than the other, to admit the line. Arrange the boom before attaching the lead, and tie a single knot just above the loop to prevent its slipping down. Bend on the lead with a " lark's-head " knot as illustrated. This is done by putting the loop through the eye, opening it, and bringing it over the base of the lead. To the projecting end of the boom attach 2 fathoms of fine white cotton snooding. This will be quite strong enough for mackerel, though fine hemp snooding is often employed. Instead of having a boom, the Devonshire fishermen merely tie a large loop with the snooding, which works loosely above the lead. A single gut collar, 1yd. in length, or No. 5 substitute, with a small swivel introduced between it and the snood, will complete your gear. Do not forget the swivel, as mackerel will twist up the gut and lessen its strength considerably by these tactics.

BAITS.—The best of all baits for mackerel is a thin slip cut from the bright side near the tail, and is termed a " sneed," lask, flot, fion, and other names. It is used with or without a spinner above the hook. To cut a sneed, take a freshly-caught mackerel, and scrape the bright under-skin near the tail. With a sharp knife, make a diagonal incision through the silvery skin, about 2½in. from the fork; cutting towards the tail, remove this part carefully, but you must not cut deeper than the red flesh. Lift it up on the blade of the knife, and place it, silvery side downwards, upon a slab of rough cork (see Fig. 34). Insert the hook at the smaller end, pressing it down until the barb has quite entered the cork beneath. Then withdraw the hook, and the bait will be found hanging from the bend ready for casting overboard. Fig. 35 shows the usual spinner with single hook baited in this way, the best hooks being the tinned Limerick variety, Nos. 1 or 1½. Sometimes a tri-

angle is used, with a longer spinner above; but a small
sneed is generally affixed to one of the hooks of the
triangle as soon as a mackerel can be caught. If you
have not a spinner in the boat, a piece of clay tobacco
pipe-stem will do instead. Whip on a hook to single

Fig. 34.—How to Bait with Sneed. The
point of the hook is inserted at the tail
part of the bait and pressed downwards
into the cork below.

gut, and pass it through the hole in the pipe-stem until
the latter rests upon the shank up to the bend. A piece
of white kid glove, a long strip of any white fish's skin, or
a gull's feather will prove useful in an emergency. The
"Dazzle" spinner (Fig. 35A) is one of the best for
mackerel. The baby-spinner is another capital bait,

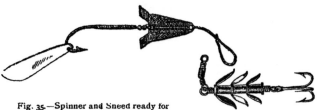

Fig. 35.—Spinner and Sneed ready for
attaching to cast (this is generally
done, however, before baiting).

Fig. 35A.—The "Dazzle '
Spinner.

with two or three white flies attached at intervals of
about 18in. When mackerel are plentiful, two or
three fish may be hauled up at once. Do not com-
mence to haul in immediately on feeling a bite, but
wait until there is a heavy pull upon the line, indicating that there are more fish than one at the end.
Fig. 36 shows the best method of attaching a fly to the

D

cast, but they are also tied on single gut. Another
good plan is to tie the loop over the knot, leaving
one-half above and one-half below.   In landing two
or three mackerel at a time, grasp the gut just above
the last fish with the left hand, the right hand being
higher up.   Always haul in a mackerel steadily, and,
taking hold of the snood as short as possible, swing the
fish carefully into the boat.   Never allow the fish to
knock against the side of the boat, or the hook may
become released by the shock.   I have seen many a
fish lost by this piece of negligence.

Fig. 36.—Mackerel Fly, showing method of attachment. The gut is
passed over the cast and the fly put through the loop.

There are no proper grounds for mackerel, as these
fish are generally scattered about over a wide area,
and anywhere in a sheltered bay may be tried.
Usually these fish come towards our shores from their
winter retreats quite early in the year, and are most
abundant perhaps during May and June.   Mackerel may
be captured with a rod from rocks and piers, using
pieces of fresh fish, small sand-eels, peeled shrimp,
or rag-worm bait.   A small sneed or the white rim
of a mussel is also highly recommended.   The Isle of
Man is an excellent locality for mackerel, and on one
occasion the extraordinary catch of over ninety dozen
was taken off this coast by one boat.   So fast was the
sport that as soon as one fish was unhooked another
had struck one of the other lines, which occasioned
continuous hauling.   I have sometimes taken one

hundred fish in the space of two or three hours, using
four lines overboard at the same time.

METHOD OF FISHING.—As soon as your line is ready,
pay out the snooding and then lower the lead until
about five fathoms of line has been let out.   Sail
should be trimmed to keep the boat moving about five
miles an hour, which can generally be managed even in
a strong breeze by taking in a reef or two or shortening
sail.   Cruise about until you have discovered a " scull "
of the fish, then go about, and return over the same
ground again.   In a light breeze pay out less line, and
use a lead of 1lb. or 1½lb. in weight should you find
that the fish are near the surface.   Two lines, one on
each side of the boat, will usually be enough for the
amateur; but professional " plummeters " use as many
as four, the extra ones being attached to "outriggers."
These are merely long poles, or spare oars, so fixed that
they project one from each quarter of the boat.   A
separate piece of cord is attached to each line, which
enables it to be hauled in from time to time to ascer-
tain whether a mackerel has seized either of the baits.
The early morning or the evening is the best time for
this sport, but mackerel can also be taken in numbers
during the day.   When fishing near the coast, pollack
may often be captured from a sailing boat, using the
same kind of tackle with spinning-eels or mackerel-
sneeds.   The boat must proceed more slowly for this
style, and a longer line should be let out.   At the
Land's End very large coal-fish and pollack are taken
in this manner, and the fishermen there use bell-wire
at the end of their lines armed with a large hook.
Whiffing from a small boat is, however, much better
than railing, for if you should hook the bottom with
the latter mode, in all probability you will lose your
gear.   When trying for pollack, always fish over rocky
ground.   As a rule the flood-tide is to be preferred
for mackereling.

BASKET.—The best basket to bring with you is one
of those close-woven square ones, with a stout handle.

Divide off a narrow portion of it with a piece of thin
board, and the space so cut off will do for your line,
tackle, knife, and other articles.   Mackerel make a
great mess in the boat if not put immediately into some
receptacle, and should be killed at once with a blow at the
back of the head.

CHAPTER VII.

LONG-LINE AND NIGHT FISHING.

TO those who dwell by the sea, the long-line
method of fishing yields endless amusement—not alone
amusement, but also instruction—for it brings to the
surface strange creatures of the marine world of all
sorts and sizes, especially if the line be set in some wild
locality like the Cornish coast or the west coast of
Ireland.   In such districts, a well-set line say, about
two miles from the shore, and with about sixty hooks,
sometimes yields to the delighted fisherman (if he be
a naturalist) specimens of the rarest, and, in many
instances, of hitherto unknown deep-sea life, curious
creatures never seen in museum or market, and which
could never be caught in nets, by reason of their being
" deep-bottom " dwellers.   To the lover of natural
history, the hauling in of a deep-sea line is a source
of the greatest excitement and pleasure.   Nor are this
excitement and pleasure confined to the contemplation
of the fish so taken; the opening of such fish, and the
discovery of various specimens of minute and beautiful
members of the Crustacea and Mollusca in their entrails
is a supreme delight in itself.   And now let me advise
those who care for the glorious study of natural history
never to allow any large fish to remain unopened, if it
be in their power to investigate its interior.   Big
fish—particularly the cod—invariably contain minute
members of the crab family, together with microscopic
Mollusca, which are well worth collecting.   The most
exquisite specimen of Dame Nature's handiwork I ever

beheld was a small crab taken from a cod-fish. It resembled, in the most remarkable manner, a delicate pink Dresden china brooch, spotted here and there with blue.

SAND-LINE.—This description of line is used on sandy beaches—localities in which the tide recedes, leaving acres of flat, sandy strand. In such places the line can be planted by simply walking out a given distance, and placing the sinker—which should be a large stone—on the sand, with one end of the line attached. Then walk towards the shore, paying out the line as you proceed, fastening the shore end to some stout, stationary object. The advancing tide soon covers your line, and the fish, following the tide, get hooked one by one, and remain struggling till the water recedes again, leaving them high and dry, awaiting your coming. This style of fishing is best followed in unfrequented places, otherwise there is the chance of the line being stolen, either before the tide comes in, or after it " goes out," unless it is constantly watched. For instance, such a mode of fishing would never pay at Ramsgate or Margate. It is perhaps best to wait by the line and haul it up as soon as the tide has attained its full height. One or two small stones should be placed at intervals along the line to keep it straight. Sometimes a large bass will take one of the lower hooks soon after they have been baited; by wading in, the fish may be unhooked and a fresh bait put on.

Now for the mode of constructing a sand-line. The one I have generally found the most useful has been 300yds. long, and fitted with fifty round-bent tinned hooks, No. 3/0, each fastened (as in Fig. 12) to 18in. of white cord, or hemp-snooding. A 40-fathom line will often be quite sufficient on a beach where the tide does not recede very far. Leave about 4ft. between each snood, and the same distance between the last hook and sinker, which should be a stone weighing about 28lb. This could be attached by twine to your main line, so that if you wanted to haul at high-water, it would break and leave the stone behind. Some-

times—even minus sinkers, and especially if the
sea has been at all rough—the line will be found
covered a foot deep in sand; but the tackle which holds
a fish is all right above ground. Your sinker is sure
to have disappeared, and you will require a spade to
dig it out. If you do not care for this trouble, your
plan is to secure sinker to line by 6ft. of "white cord,"
which you can cut if you find your sinker *non est.* Bait
your hooks alternately with sand-launce, mud-worm, lugs,
and whelk. If your line is set in a "pleasant place,"
you ought to be rewarded by at least forty fish, com-
prising codling, flounder, mullet, turbot, and other
sandy-bottom rovers. If you possess a boat, you can,
of course, row out when the tide is full, and haul in,
unhook, re-bait, and set again, thus having two catches
in one tide. This mode of fishing requires two to work
properly. The line should be neatly coiled in a shallow
tub, or vessel of that description, the hooks being
arranged in the centre of the coil; one person should
hold the tub as the other pays out the line. Always
get a supply of bait—sand-launce is best—beforehand,
as you will not have time when the tide is rising.

Another and better plan is to deposit your line at
low-water, but, instead of laying it up and down the
beach, place it as near as possible to the waves and
parallel with them, bringing the main line—which is
unfurnished with hooks—above high-water mark. Thus,
the whole of the baits will be quickly covered, and, as
they will all remain in deep water, larger fish will
consequently be caught. There should be a stone
fastened to each end of the baited portion. Spring-
tides are the best for this amusement.

CIRCUS, OR "TRAVELLER."—This is another style of
line used in strand-fishing, and has the advantage of
being easily managed by one person. The following is
the mode of using it: Attach a small iron or brass ring
to a large stone, by lashing it on with stout cord (see
Fig. 37), and place this about a hundred yards out on
the sands. Have a 300ft. length of line, with about
thirty spiller hooks, each on 2ft. of white cord snooding.

Fasten them near the centre of the line, and at 4ft.
apart. Fasten one end of the line on the shore, run
the other end through the ring on the stone, and walk
back to shore carrying the line with you. Now you
have both ends of the line at your feet, while the ring
allows you to pull in the hooks and pull them out to
sea again, so that you can haul in as often as you like
during the tide. Tie a piece of stick between the last
hook, or, rather, the first hook and ring, to keep the
former from slipping through the latter. Bait as for
sand-line fishing.

Fig. 37.—Mode of Arranging Circus Line to Ring on Sinker, showing
piece of wood which acts as a stop when the line is hauled out.

DEEP-SEA LINE.—This is the line which the naturalist
loves to watch as it is being hauled in; but to use it
properly you must have a good boat, with a comfort-
able width of beam, and a companion who knows the
art of managing a boat as well as fishing. A wild,
rocky coast is the best of all localities for deep-sea-
fishing. Bulters are generally used by professionals,
these are long lines exceedingly strong, bearing sometimes as many as 500 hooks. Ordinary cod-hooks are
the proper size, and they are fastened to strong snoods,
about 18in. long, made of several strands of fine twine.
This is passed around a hook or other fixture with a
netting-needle, and two half-hitches made on the
shank at each turn, the snood being afterwards

"marled down," leaving a large loop at the end. Sometimes they are protected by copper-wire for a short distance above the hook. The snoods are attached to the backing at regular intervals apart, which are always double the length of each snood. Buoys and anchors are employed to moor the bulter, and they are shot in deep water on " marks" well known to the local fishermen.

Spillering is capital amusement for the amateur, the " spiller," as it is called, being more convenient, and is, in reality, only a bulter on a small scale. All kinds of fish, such as turbot, plaice, gurnards, bass, pollack, and cod, may be taken with them, and hauling in such a line always creates much excitement, especially

Fig. 38.—Rig for Spiller Snoods (a brass sheave with copper wire twisted around the groove and swivel).

amongst the young people. Fig. 38 depicts an excellent invention for keeping the snood from fouling the main line, or spiller " back." It is a round brass sheave, with a hole in the centre, through which the line passes, and any ironmonger would supply them. It should revolve quite loosely upon the main line, the hole being enlarged for that purpose. Place two or three turns of lead-wire on either side to keep it in its position. Pass a piece of stout copper-wire around the groove, and, having made an eye in the longer end and inserted a swivel, twist the two ends together. Stout conger-line should constitute the spiller " back," and the hooks— No. 3/0, round-bend—to the number of 100 to 150, are each attached to pieces of stout snooding 18in. in length. The end of each is then fastened to the eye of a swivel. To keep the hooks and snoods from becoming entangled, an arrangement for keeping them separate, such as that shown in Fig. 43, must be provided. A useful holder for spillering is formed like a comb, having four prongs, over which to pass the hooks. Besides the main line, you will require two buoy-ropes, one for each end of the line, and two large stones to serve as anchors. The buoys are made of fishing-cork, and several pieces are placed one on the top of the other, with a small flag in the centre (see

Fig. 39.—Marks and Killick, showing method of bending on the stone. A small flag attached to a piece of cane is fixed into the topmost cork.

Fig. 39) for discovering the whereabouts of your "marks." Attach the stones as shown in the drawing; this is the "killick bend," and an excellent plan for mooring a small boat for ground-fishing. To make this fastening, take the end of the rope, pass it round the main part, and twist it several times, forming a large loop. Pass this over the centre of stone, and make a half-hitch alongside it.

The best baits for spillering are pieces of fresh fish, such as pilchard, herring, or mackerel, cut up (see Fig. 17). Sand-eels, strips of cuttle, or whelks are also

much esteemed.   For turbot, sand-eels or smelts are
considered the best.

Adjust your hooks regularly upon the holder, which,
for convenience, should be fixed into the gunwale of the
boat.   Bait each hook in turn, and when baited, coil
the line carefully in a large square basket, leaving the
hooks on one side separate from the main line.   Attach
one end of your spiller just above one of the stones,
and when arrived upon the ground, lower away carefully, paying out the line, and seeing that each hook
goes out clear.   Your companion should meanwhile
row slowly in the proper direction.   Lower the second
stone similarly to the first, and cast out the corks.   Provide plenty of rope for the depth in which you want
to " shoot."

The entrance to harbours is a good place to set a
spiller, or in any sandy cove near the edge of the rocks.
Shoot across the tide, and do not leave the spiller down
more than an hour.   Always provide a strong gaff and
a knife in the boat.   Flood-tide is the best time for
spillering, and it can be followed in the daytime.
Bultering is generally carried on by night, hauling the
following morning.

NIGHT-FISHING.—This is a style of fishing to which
I confess to being very partial, although, as a rule, it
is not very enthusiastically followed by unprofessional
fishermen, it being thought a rather dangerous pastime.
As far as I am concerned, I have never experienced any
danger while night-fishing, and think it far safer than
many other amusements, such as hunting, steeple-
chasing, shooting with a nervous, unpractised companion, &c.   The principal danger is popularly sup-
posed to lie in the chance of being run down by some
trawler, barque, or steamer.   This danger, however, is
easily guarded against by having a brilliant red lamp
on a pole, and keeping a good look-out.   Always have
at least two " good and true " companions, and, above
all, a stout seaworthy boat.   See that your anchor and
anchor-lines are stout and strong.   The biggest fish
feed by night, and, should you be on good ground, you

will have plenty of sport. Use similar line and tackle as for day-fishing, but with stronger snoods. Bait with sand-launce, cuttle, or pieces of fresh fish. Start for the fishing-ground in good time, so that you will be able to see the "marks" while the daylight lasts (see "Taking Marks," Chapter III.).

Almost every variety of hand-lining and long line-laying has been described, but there are one or two modes especially adapted to sandy shores, which were described by the late Mr. E. R. Suffling (author of "The Land of the Broads") some years ago in *The Exchange and Mart*; and, as the information given is very useful, I cannot do better than republish his remarks *in extenso*. The writer says: "Mr. Hudson, in his articles, speaks of the 'traveller, or circus line,' and

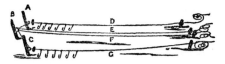

Fig 40.—Double Out-haul for Codling, stakes having been driven into the sand, with staples for hauling in the lines.

gives an illustration (Fig. 37) showing the line rove through a loop attached to a stone sinker or rock-anchor, a contrivance which is very simple, but has the drawback of being very liable to foul. The out-haul line, with its hooks, frequently becomes entangled with the other line, and causes much annoyance, and, at times, brings the fishing to an abrupt conclusion.

"Fig. 40 shows an improved method of 'out-haul-fishing,' a method in use on the East Coast for catching codling. It is extremely simple, and is managed in this way: Three stout stakes, about 6ft. long, are procured, and pointed at the lower end, and an iron staple driven into each of them about 2ft. from the top. At low-water these stakes are driven into the sand, leaving about 3ft. protruding above the surface. They are placed at each angle of an imaginary triangle, about

10ft. or 12ft. apart, with the staples facing towards tne shore.   The lines (D and G) are passed through the staples in the posts A and C, then through the staple in post B, and back to the shore, as shown at E and F.   By this arrangement they are kept wide enough apart to prevent any possibility of the hooks fouling, and the lines with the hooks may be hauled in either singly or both at the same time if the fish are felt upon them. To prevent the hooks being drawn through the staples, a piece of wood, about 3in. long, is fastened to the line 4ft. in advance of the outermost hook.

"To keep the lines fairly taut, so as not to be fouled by the set of a strong tide, it will be found necessary to drive four short stakes into the beach just above high-water mark, to which to belay the ends of the lines.

Fig. 41.—Ever-baited Traveller, showing one set of hooks hauled out as far as the stake whilst the other set is inshore.

The fisherman, by taking the lines D and G in his hand occasionally, can easily detect the presence of a codling on any of the hooks by a peculiar tremulous movement of the line which there is no mistaking.   When a fish is felt, the line should immediately be hauled in rapidly but quietly, not in spasmodic jerks, or the hook, if not fairly home in the codling's maw, may be jerked out and the fish lost.   Codling are very fond of sprats, but will take the lug-worm greedily.   On the East Coast the season is from October to March.

"When the fish are close in, and feeding, they may, at times, be caught very quickly; so, to save time, I have adopted the scheme shown in Fig. 41, which I have called the 'ever-baited traveller.'   At this name I beg the reader will not laugh; for, although a matter of fun to him, it has proved a matter of death to some scores of poor, confiding codling.

"A glance at the drawing will explain its working. Two stakes (A and B), fitted with staples, are driven into the sand at dead low tide—the farther out the better—a line passed through the two staples, and the two ends carried well above high-water mark. Six or eight hooks are then placed on the line close to the stake B, with a wooden stop 4ft. from the outermost, to prevent the hooks going too near the staple. Then, towards the other end of the line, fastened to a peg, just above high-water mark, six or eight more hooks are affixed, also with a wooden stop in front of them. Now, when the tide is about half-flood, fishing may be commenced, and as the first flight of hooks is hauled in, the fish taken off, and the hooks examined to see that the baits are intact, the other flight is hauled out to stake A, so that no time is lost, and thus a single line does the duty

Fig. 42.—Tripping-line (A) attached to flukes of anchor for raising it from the sand.

of two. Pegs driven in the sand will keep the shore-ends of the line from being washed away by the current, which, during the rise of the tide, is usually very strong.

"The hooks should be ordinary codling-hooks, upon snoods of water-cord, about 15in. long, and should have a distance of 3ft. between them when placed on the line. Skate and flat-fish of all kinds will also be captured beside the codling. A dark night with a little 'popple' on the sea is the best time to choose for this kind of amusement. As bait for codling, nothing can be used with greater success than lug-worms, failing which, sprats or big shrimps may be tried. Pieces of any other fish, cut into short strips, are also used; but, whatever form of bait is used, it must be sweet and fresh, as the codling is a much cleaner feeder than any other fish—the conger, for example.

"After the tide has fallen about an hour, very few

fish will be taken, as they draw out with the receding
tide into deeper water.

" When a long line is laid, say, 200yds. from shore,
at dead water, and anchored at each end with a small
anchor, it is often required to haul the line at high-
water. For that purpose, a tripping-line (A, Fig. 42)
is attached to the anchor at the junction of the flukes

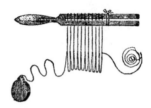

Fig. 43.—Hook-holder, with hooks arranged upon it to prevent
entanglement.

and shank, and the other end taken ashore ; then, upon
pulling at the tripping-line, the anchor is hauled
ashore *backwards,* with the line of hooks fastened to it.

" Amateur fishermen often get into a sad state of
tangle with their hooks, which has the effect of ruffling
their otherwise placid temperaments. To avoid this, a
very simple contrivance (Fig. 43) may be made out of a

Fig. 44.—Section of Holder, showing plan for reception of hook.

piece of hard wood, 12in. long and 1in. square. First
round up the wood, with a pocket-knife or rasp, for a
length of 4in., to form a handle; then, from the other
end, make a broad saw-cut 7in. long, and smooth it
with a flat file. The piece of wood will then appear
with an end view like that shown in Fig. 44, except
that one side must be rounded as shown, and a hollow
scooped out along the outside. Into this hollow the

barb of the hook should fit. To use this instrument, it is merely necessary to slip the shank of the hook along the slot in the wood with the bend of the hook over the rounded portion. The whole slot may thus be filled up with hooks to the number of forty or fifty without the least fear of entanglement. If only a few hooks are placed on this handy little holder, a piece of twine should be tied round to keep them from slipping off. The line is best wound on a wooden cross, made with a pointed foot or arm for sticking in the sand, and with a loop at the top for hanging up (see Fig. 45).

Fig. 45.—Holder for Line, with the lower end pointed for thrusting into the sand.

" A new line should always be stretched before using, directions for which have already been given in Chapter I.

" All visitors to the seaside are familiar with the little spiral heaps of sand thrown up by lug-worms on the sandy foreshore below high-water mark. But of all these visitors, how many of them could capture half-a-dozen of these creatures in an hour, even if provided with a spade? Very few, I am sure, unless they knew how to set about it, for at the least movement of the sand the lug-worm darts down the hole which it has already provided as a means of escape, and, with lightning rapidity, is out of reach of its would-be

captor. With a little care, however, ten out of twelve
ought to be taken. A long, narrow, clay-spade is
necessary to dig them out with. I have endeavoured
to show the manner of digging by the accompanying
diagram (Fig. 46). A little distance from the 'put,'
or 'coil,' as it is called, dig a trench by removing about
four spadefuls (1, 2, 3, 4) of sand, the full depth of
the spade; then take a good deep slice off at 5, so that
only a distance of 2in. separates the 'put' from the
trench. Now is the crucial time, as on the next delve of
the spade depends the success or non-success of the effort.
With a very rapid thrust, send the spade down 7in. or

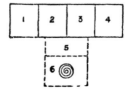

Fig. 46.—Diagram showing manner of Digging for Lug-worms. Four
spadefuls are removed as shown, then the upper portion of No. 5 is
thrown out, and finally the worm is unearthed at the "cast" (No. 6).

8in. behind the 'put'(6), and throw out the sand with a
forward motion, which will have the effect of turning
the tail of the worm at right angles from you, thus: ⌐.
He is now yours, as, when his tail is once turned from
the perpendicular, he cannot descend his hole. You
have then merely to thrust your spade down under
him another 6in., and you bring him to light—a huge,
hairy, red-and-yellow beast, frequently 9in. long, and
as thick as one's fore-finger. There is no finer bait
than this worm; but it has one drawback, namely, that
it stains the fingers a bright yellow, which takes a
day or two to erase. If the fisherman be afraid of the
'golden fingers,' he had better don a pair of ordinary
hedging-gloves, which will cost about 1s.
  "The simplest and most come-at-able buoys for sea-
fishing purposes are either an inflated bullock's bladder

or a large Australian meat-tin, with the lid re-soldered on. The latter makes a very efficient buoy, as it will stand any amount of rough usage. A ring should be soldered on one end, to which to attach the line, and nothing better can be needed. The tin should be painted white or bright vermilion, so as to be readily seen when the night is dark. If it be coated with a luminous paint, so much the better." This can be obtained through almost any ironmonger, with brush and full instructions how to apply it.

CHAPTER VIII.

LOBSTERS, CRABS, AND CRAWFISH.

THE lobster is, beyond all question, the most delicious of the Crustacea, though, strange to say, those very dainty epicures, the ancient Romans, did not seem to esteem it highly, but went in heavily for crab and crawfish, the latter, served with divers herbs and sauces, being a standing dish of honour at their banquets. Even in this present century of enlightenment, I have known people who have not hesitated in ranking the crawfish first in the list of his family. But, then, there are people who prefer mussels to oysters, and flounders to soles. Such oddities are, however, in the minority. Were I required to draw out a list of the edible members of the Crustacea, and to place each according to its rank, I would do so as follows: 1, lobster; 2, Dublin prawn; 3, crab; 4, crawfish; 5, English prawn; 6, shrimp.

The Dublin (sometimes called Dublin Bay) prawn was, until some time after the war, very little known in England, but it is now quite common in the better sort of fishmongers and has become a much appreciated delicacy. It measures, on an average, about 9in. from the tip of its claw to the end of its tail. It is very much like a lobster

E

in shape, but with narrow, elongated, serrated, pink-tinted
claws. These prawns are sold in England during the
season at about 1½d. each, and half a dozen make an
abundant meal.

Our coasts yield an abundant harvest of shell-fish,
and even in Ireland, where the common London
shrimp seems to be unknown, and the crawfish almost
so, there are lobsters and crabs galore. But, still, our
coasts are simply barren in comparison with those of

Fig. 47.—"Jack's" Bag-net, with three cords for slinging it.

Southern Europe and the tropics. Indeed, the warmer
the latitude the more plentiful the variety of shell-
fish. The shores of Japan teem with dozens of different specimens of the crab family alone, and round
the coral islands dwell crawfish which reach nearly
3ft. in length. Our gallant tars, when quartered in
such happy hunting-grounds, have rare sport with our
shelly friends, especially with the crawfish, which does
not seem to be quite so nervous and retiring in its
habits as the lobster.

Jack's favourite mode of fishing is to fasten a piece of netting to an iron hoop, thus making a capital bag-net (Fig. 47), which, after baiting with fish-offal or salt-pork, and attaching a stone for a sinker, he lowers over the side of the ship. In a few minutes he hauls it up again, and is generally rewarded with one or more crawfish, and sometimes by a couple of lobsters and crabs. This net is very similar to the baited prawn-net (Fig. 51), of which particulars are given in the next chapter, except that the hoop should be rather larger. Some of these nets have a ring 6ft. or more in diameter, and for taking lobsters they can hardly be too large. They may be set in the same manner as the baited prawn-net, using sufficient corks to buoy the rope, or lowered over the side of a pier.

On parts of the American coast, where the lobsters do not appear to stick so close to sunken rocks and deep water, there is a method of catching them which, I believe, is called by our cousins "lobster-pinning." A long pole, with a narrow, forked end is procured, and is used from a boat in shallow water. When a lobster is seen, the pole is slowly lowered right over him, and then, with a sudden dart, he is pinned between the fork, and hoisted on board. But this mode of fishing is scarcely practicable in our British waters, where the lobster is not very often to be tackled at close quarters.

The lobster is a most prolific fish, the female producing something like 20,000 eggs in the season. These are the "coral," in which epicures so much delight. Now that the trade is so enormous, the constant catching of female lobsters with eggs must gradually decrease the numbers round our coasts. The by-laws usually prohibit the removal of "berried" lobsters, or those carrying spawn. I have seen it stated that, on some days during the season, as many as 25,000 lobsters reach Billingsgate alone, all of which have been caught round our coasts.

Lobster and Crab Pot.—Fig. 48 represents the kind most commonly used by fishermen around our coasts, and usually composed of osiers or willows woven

together. Some are made of galvanised iron, but are
not so good as the former. The bars could easily be
made closer by weaving wire or cord around them,
though the more open they are the better the fish can
see the contents when baited. Still, it is sometimes
necessary to have them a little closer when such fish
as small conger glide in, and, having gobbled up all
the bait, glide serenely out again. Professionals
usually make their own pots during the winter months.

Fig. 48.—Crab-pot and Buoy-rope as they should appear when properly
set, the pot being weighted at the bottom with flat stones.

The best kind has a removable bottom, attached to the
upper portion by galvanised iron wire. By detaching the
bottoms, the pots can be stowed away one on the top of
the other. The buoy-rope is attached to the bottom, as
illustrated, by which method the crab-pot offers less re-
sistance to the water when hauled up, though some professionals fasten it to the sides.

LOBSTER-CATCHING.—The lobster never goes far from
its favourite rocks, being extremely local in its habits;
consequently, some judgment must be exercised in
" shooting " your pot. If you can, by any fortunate

chance, discover the whereabouts of any narrow channel between two ledges of sunken rocks, there you will secure the largest lobsters and crawfish. Bait your pot with fish-offal (the head of a cod fish is a deadly bait), securing such by pegging it to the bottom of the pot with sharp pieces of stick, thrust in through the bars; also place a heavy flat stone or two in the pot, to act as sinkers. A stale bait is said to be the best for catching a lobster, and all kinds of fish are used, cut up into pieces. Row out to the spot you have fixed on for " shooting " your pot, and lower it by strong buoy-line, to which you must affix a large bunch of corks painted white, as a mark of its whereabouts. Professionals cut their initials in large letters upon the top cork to identify their gear in case it should be cast away in a gale of wind. Crab-pots are usually hauled at low-water slack tide. At high-water the corks are often "under-run," or submerged, and cannot be picked up. If you are in a neighbourhood where lobster and crab-catching is followed by the natives as a means of livelihood, you had better set your pot after dark, and haul it up ere sunrise; or you can anchor the boat beside it, and amuse yourself by hand-line fishing, raising your pot every half-hour or so, until you are tired of the sport for one day.

CRAB-CATCHING.—There are several methods adopted, the commonest (and best) being by the " crab-pot." A similar kind of pot and bait to that employed for catching lobsters is required, and the fish abound in the same locality. Crabs prefer fresh bait, rays being frequently utilised for this purpose. Even the best fish, such as turbot, are sometimes cut up for bait, the crabber's maxim being: " The better the bait, the better the fish." The male, or " he "-crab, is the one which is valued for eating, and can be readily recognised from the female by the greater size of its claws. When crabs are removed from the pot, their claws are " nicked," to prevent their biting or killing one another, which consists of cutting the muscle at the junction

of the two parts of the claw with a sharp knife.
Lobsters and crabs are kept in "store-pots," anchored
near the shore, until they are required for sale. Always
weigh a crab in your hand before you buy him, and
only by this means can you tell whether he has been
freshly caught. The inside may have shrunk considerably, and the crab have lost much weight; but the outside shell will always remain the same. These shell-
fish should be punctured with some sharp instrument,
and then placed into absolutely boiling water, in which
case they speedily die. Much unnecessary cruelty is
practised by putting them into cold water, and then
placing the saucepan upon the fire.

On some parts of our coasts, "crab-hooking" is practised, but I do not recommend that method to novices;
it requires a lot of practice to become an expert at
this business, which is conducted as follows: When a
spring-tide makes a "great out," and low-lying rocks
are exposed to man's gaze, the crab-hooker, armed with
a long pole, to which an iron crook is fastened, makes
his way over the slimy rocks, heedless of an occasional
fall, and inserts the crook into every hole and under
every ledge he comes across. It requires the practised
hand to distinguish the crab from any other object
with which the crook may come in contact. When the
crab is felt, it must be crooked out on the instant; for,
if once it "gets its back up," it will resist every effort
to remove it, and will allow the crook to tear it into
bits.

CRAWFISH-CATCHING.—This fish is frequently taken
by hand-line when rocky-bottom fishing, and with
hooks baited with herring or whelk. You can easily
tell when you have one by the steady pull and absence
of "wriggle." You must pull in the line very steadily,
or, the instant the crawfish comes to the top of the
water, it will let go if you are not quick enough to
catch it by one of its long feelers. The crawfish is
a coarser-grained fish than its cousins, the lobster and
crab, but when properly cooked does not make a very
bad substitute for either. Numbers of crawfish are

taken in trammels, and I have seen specimens weighing over 9lb. captured in this way. These fish become entangled in the net by their claws or legs, and are unable to free themselves. Edible crabs also become meshed in the nets, but they create great havoc with the twine, and often succeed in eating their way out, and getting clear away.

A good deal of practice is required in removing lobsters and crabs from a pot; but if you grasp the former by the back, they cannot hurt you. Crabs are held in the same way by the back portion of the upper shell, which renders them incapable of reaching the hand with their powerful front claws. The lobster is dark blue in colour when alive, but becomes red after it has been boiled.

CHAPTER IX.

SHRIMPS AND PRAWNS.

LIKE the crab, lobster, and crawfish, the shrimp and prawn are to be met with in all parts of the world, and in warm latitudes the latter reaches a very large size—much larger than even the Dublin prawn—specimens having been taken over a foot in length. The common English shrimp of commerce is found on almost every part of our coasts, and, like the crab and lobster, affords a means of livelihood to thousands of fishermen. The quantity of shrimps and prawns consumed in London daily, during the season, must be counted by the billion.

The prawn is frequently confounded with the shrimp, but in reality they are two different species. Small prawns are often wrongly termed "shrimps," whereas the latter are grey, and in their natural state this colour assimilates remarkably with the sand or mud upon which they are found. On the other hand, the prawn, of whatever size, is transparent yellow when

alive, only becoming red after being boiled. It also
possesses a kind of sword, or spear, projecting from the
head, which is almost entirely absent in the shrimp.
Prawns delight in rocky places, where there is a quantity of seaweed under which they can lie concealed, but
shrimps prefer mud or sand.

DREDGE-NET FISHING.—Shrimps and prawns are
often found on flat sandy ground, and, consequently,
are easily caught by dredge-nets; these can be pur-
chased through any fishing-tackle manufacturer. Such
a description of net affords great amusement, for not
only will it bring up shrimps and prawns to the surface,
but also small soles, flounders, and fish of that class.
Always return the latter to the sea again and allow

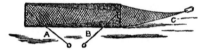

Fig. 49.—Dredge-net, fitted with two iron bars (A, B) for drawing it,
C being the purse of the net tied with twine.

them to grow larger, as they are practically useless for
food.   The illustration (Fig. 49) represents the net in
question. The mouth of the net, which is oblong, and
varies from 10in. to 2ft. in width, by 6in. to 9in. deep,
is composed of flat iron about 3in. wide.   In order that
the outer edge shall keep close to the bottom, it is made
to project outwards, the inner opening being a little
smaller.   To this is attached a net of stout twine,
tapering towards the other end.   The two iron bars
(A and B) are hinged on to the frame, which is
also of iron.   A drag rope—length according to
depth of water—is fastened to the two bars,
the other end being secured to a peg or other object in
the boat. The net is lowered over the side of the boat,
which is rowed very slowly. As the boat moves, it, of
course, drags the iron-framed net along the sandy
bottom.   By the way, I should mention that the

net itself has an opening in the bottom (at
c), which is tied up with a piece of strong twine
until hauled up, when, on loosening the twine,
the contents of the net roll out without any bother.
This dredge is principally used by naturalists for bringing up shells, &c., from the bottom of the sea. It can
be drawn by a small sailing or motor boat in harbours
or bays, and we have used it for dredging up oysters.
Collectors might obtain many beautiful and rare shells
by this method. Shrimps and prawns can be captured
in greater numbers by using a small trawl specially
constructed for the purpose, but this method is pro-
hibited in some waters. All kinds of gear for this sport
can be obtained from Messrs. Hearder and Son, 195,
Union Street, Plymouth.

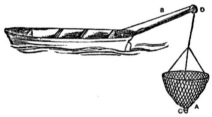

Fig. 50.—Bag-net worked with Crane (D) and Pulley-rope (B). The
bottom of net (A) is tied up with twine at C.

BAG-NET FISHING.—There is a mode of catching eels
which is adopted by fishermen in Ireland, and which,
I think, might be practised with advantage by both professional and amateur shrimp and prawn catchers round
the English coast. It consists of a round bag-net, something like the net used by sailors when fishing for
crawfish, as described in Chap. VIII., but with a purse,
or open bottom, as in the dredge-net. It is worked
from a boat by a sort of crane and pulley, as shown at
Fig. 50. The net (A) is baited with fish offal, and
lowered—by pulley rope B—to the bottom. When
hauled up again, the twine (C) is untied, and out come

the contents, as in dredge-net. The boat must be at
anchor when fishing in this manner. D represents
wheel affixed to crane on which pulley works.

BAITED PRAWN-NET.—This is another description of
net which can be used from a boat, and is sometimes
called a "float-net." They are often employed in
Devonshire, and large quantities of very fine prawns
will thus be captured. It is simply a round bag-net,
fitted with an iron hoop, ½in. thick, and 2ft. in diameter. The net, which is rather shallow, is composed

Fig. 51.—Float-net, showing how it is slung. A represents the
buoy-cork.

of strong cord, afterwards tarred to preserve it. Across
the centre of the hoop two pieces of twine, each doubled,
are fastened, the ends being attached to the rim, and
between these the bait is placed. To keep the bait in
the centre of the ring, two small pieces of leather are
threaded on the twine, one on each side, which are
pushed up against the bait. Four pieces of leather are
therefore required to hold the bait in its position.
Three stout cords are now required to suspend the hoop,
as shown in Fig. 51, and a buoy-line about 7

fathoms long, with several corks along it to keep it clear
of the net. A shows the end cork, but a reference to
Fig. 48 will afford a better idea of the rope. Bait these
nets with any kind of fresh fish you can procure, cutting
it open to render it more attractive. Prawns and lobsters
prefer stale bait. This method must be followed in the
evening about nine or ten o'clock, and you should carry
a lantern with you. Two persons should be in the boat,
and twenty or thirty nets can easily be worked by one
man. Stretch a piece of canvas loosely between the
thwarts of the boat, in which to deposit the contents.
Shoot the nets one after the other in about three or
four fathoms of water, hauling in about half-an-hour's
time. Do not attempt to separate the prawns from the
crabs, &c., but empty them all into the canvas, and sort
them afterwards. An apron should be worn. A large
basketful of prawns is often taken by one boat in a
single evening, and the best time is late summer or
autumn. Two or three of these boats are often lowered
from a quay-side.

At low water a similar kind of net can be used
amongst rocks, and there is no need for a boat. Immediately above the junction of the three cords the main
line should be reeved through the centre of a round
flat bung, two others being similarly placed above and
at a distance of 1ft. apart. The net is made quite
shallow in the centre, but has two pockets at the sides,
about 6in. deep, into which the prawns find their way.
The top cork should be painted white to be more easily
discerned, and four of these nets will be quite enough
to work properly. Provide a pole, about 12ft. long,
with a fork at the end resembling a pitch-fork, for
raising or lowering them. Bait with small crabs or
limpets by transfixing them upon thin wooden skewers.
These should be then passed between the meshes of the
net, the ends being across the shallow part. Deposit the
nets wherever seems a likely place, leaving them down
a few minutes, then raise them steadily by means of the
long pole. The evening is the best time, commencing
about two hours before low water.

HAND-NET FISHING.—Armed with the strand-net
shown at Fig. 52, the fisherman wades into the water,
pushing the net before him, until he thinks there is
something in it, when he raises it, takes out the contents, which he places in a basket slung across the
shoulders, and then has another try. This method is
generally employed by professionals, and can be only
practised successfully on mud or sand.   The best
time to shrimp is at low-water spring-tide, especially

Fig. 52.—Strand-net, fitted with handle, for shrimping on mud or sand in
shallow water.

when the water has commenced to flow. Wear a pair
of long waterproof boots, reaching to the thigh, and
push the net along, making the front bar scrape the
bottom.   Having thus proceeded for some distance,
return to shore and empty all the catch upon the sand,
picking out the prawns from amongst the seaweed. An
old fishing-basket is the best receptacle for them, fastened by a strap across the shoulders, as this leaves both
hands free. In harbours or near piers are good places
to try, provided there are not many rocks to obstruct
the progress of the net.

Pool-Net.—This is much more handy than the strand-net, and a great favourite with shrimp and prawn-catchers both young and old. Procure an iron hoop, from 12in. to 16in. in diameter, and ⅜in. thick, from a blacksmith. The two ends must be forged together into a spike (see Fig. 53) with which to fix it into the handle. This is a light pole, 6ft. or 7ft. long,

Fig 53.—Hoop for Pool-net, the two ends forged into a spike for driving into handle.

and an ordinary broom-handle, obtainable from any ironmonger, would answer. A brass ferrule should be driven on to one end to prevent the wood splitting. Bore a hole exactly in the centre, and having heated the spike red-hot drive it into the handle up to the ring. Some pool-nets have the ring elliptical in shape,

Fig. 54.—Pool-net complete with handle.

and the iron of the hoop is flattened, holes being bored in it about 2in. apart for attaching the net. I have always found about 14in. in diameter the handiest size for the ring, and the net should be composed of No. 18 Irish flax netting thread, obtainable from Messrs. Wm. Good and Son, Ltd., 46, Fish Street Hill, Monument, London, E.C. 3. Lace on the net with copper wire or strong snooding, and the last loops should be double.

Fig. 54 shows this net complete. The best places for prawning are round the edges of rocks at low spring tides, or in pools left by the sea in which there is plenty of weed. Prawns delight in lying under the long ore-weed, which is found in abundance on some parts of our coast. Be very careful not to disturb a pool in which you intend to fish. In small pools it is usually considered a good plan to lift up all the seaweed first with the hands, when you can more easily capture the prawns by guiding them into the net. Every movement must be made with great caution, otherwise your efforts will meet with little reward. If there is a hole in the pool under a large rock, place your net in front of the opening to prevent the prawns escaping in that direction. They are especially fond of pools containing these hiding-places, into which they can retreat in times of danger.

Near a pier, prawns may often be taken in shallow water from a boat when the tide is flowing. Place the net just in front of them, when they will enter unsuspiciously, and may be lifted out. Never go about with bare feet when shrimping or prawning, but wear a pair of waterproof boots, or an old pair of sand-shoes without socks which you do not mind wetting.

To boil prawns, place them into thoroughly boiling water, adding a handful of salt, and in three minutes they will be cooked. A better plan is to boil the prawns in fresh water, and sprinkle them with salt after removal.

CHAPTER X.

SEASONS FOR DIFFERENT FISH.

I think it well to give here the names of various sea-fish to be met with during the different months of the year. Those fish which are in their finest condition for table will be found italicised under their proper months.

January.—Brill, *cod*, coal-fish, dory, eel, *haddock*, *ling*, mackerel, pout, red gurnard, shell-fish, skate, smelt, whiting.

February.—Brill, *cod, dab*, eel, ling. mackerel, pout, red gurnard, shell-fish, smelt, sprat, whiting.

March.—Brill, conger, *dab, mackerel*, pout, shell-fish, skate, smelt, sprat, turbot.

April.—*Brill*, conger, *dab*, eel, hake, *mackerel*, pout, scad, shell-fish, skate, smelt, thornback, *turbot*.

May.—Bass, brill, conger, dory, hake, launce, mackerel, mullet, pollack, scad, skate, *smelt*, turbot, wrasse.

June.—*Bass*, brill, *bream*, conger, dory, eel, *flounder*, hake, halibut, mackerel, mullet, pilchard, *plaice*, pollack, smelt, *soles.* thornback, turbot, wrasse.

July.—Bass, brill, bream, conger, dab, *flounder*, hake, halibut, launce, mullet, pilchard, *plaice*, pollack, skate, *sole*, turbot.

August.—*Bass*, bream, brill, conger, dab, *dory*, flounder, gurnard, *herring, hake,* halibut, launce, *mullet* (red and grey), *pilchard*, plaice, *pollack*, skate, sole, turbot, *whiting*.

September.—Bass, bream, coal-fish, *conger*, flounder, gurnard, *hake*, halibut, herring, *pilchard*, plaice, *pollack*, shell-fish.

October.—Brill, cod, conger, dab, flounder, gurnard, haddock, hake, halibut, mullet, pilchard, plaice, pollack, shell-fish, shad, *skate*, smelt, sole, turbot.

November.—Brill, cod, codling, dab, eel, flounder, haddock, halibut, hake, herring, ling. pilchard, plaice, *pout*, shad, shell-fish, smelt, sole, turbot.

December.—Coal-fish, cod, codling, haddock, hake, ling, mackerel, *pout*, shell-fish, skate, smelt, whiting.

The above list is only intended as a general guide, and probably some of the various sea-fish may differ in their habits according to the locality.

During the months of July and August, certain parts of the coast are visited by countless myriads of the herring-fry, which keep close to the surface of the water. They can be taken wholesale in buckets, baskets, bag-nets, or, in fact, in any utensil, by simply lowering it into the water and lifting it up again. These minute, silvery creatures, called in London "whitebait," are delicious when fried in butter; they are also a deadly bait for cod, hake, haddock—in fact, for all large fish

CHAPTER XI.

GENERAL HINTS.

IN this chapter I will call attention to some important hints, several of which have been given in the preceding pages, but which will bear repetition.

1. Never go to sea without satisfying yourself that the boat is all right and seaworthy. Do not let the brightness or calmness of the day lull your watchfulness on this point. The warmer the day, the more liable you are to be visited by a sudden squall. Never go to leeward in a small boat, otherwise, if the wind should rise, much difficulty may be experienced in returning. In small sailing craft the main-sheet should be belayed by a single turn and a bight, so that, by pulling at the end of the rope, it may be cast off at a moment's notice in case a squall should strike the sail.

Always carry an old macintosh or "oiler" with you to protect you from spray or a sudden downpour of rain.

A convenient little boat, which could be used for any class of sea-fishing, is one 13ft. 6in. long, with a good beam, and rigged with lug sail and small mizen. The ballast should be cast to fit snugly below the bottom boards. Such a boat will row and sail well, and they are much used by fishermen on the Cornish coast. For fishing some distance from land, however, a more powerful boat is advisable. Always take care that the gun-

wale of the boat is entirely free from nails. When going
out whiffing, always take a "killick," or large stone, with
you and a few fathoms of "road" (rope), so that you can
anchor if the wind and tide are against you. A leather
groin protector is very useful for resting the rod-butt while
reeling in.

A boat-mat is useful when much rowing has to be
done, and should measure 17in. by 10in. The material
should consist of coarse canvas "thrummed" with
white cotton, which could be readily washed when
dirty. Attach it to the thwart by pieces of tape, sewn
on to each end. Cushions are also used for this purpose.

Fig. 55.—Gaff-hook with spike at bottom, and the same fitted into handle.

2. GAFFS.—Fig. 55 shows a capital gaff, with the
method of fixing it into the handle. It should be made
of the best steel, carefully tempered, about ⅜in.
thick near the base, and 3in. in width from the point
across the curve measuring from the outside. The
bottom is furnished with a spike as shown, which, after
being passed through a hole in the handle, is clenched
at the back. A brass ferrule is afterwards passed over
the point and holds it firmly. The handle is 2ft. 10in.
long and made of ash, and may be provided with a knob
at the end for conger-fishing. It should be varnished
with two coats of yacht spar varnish to keep out the wet.
A common gaff could be made by lashing a large conger
hook to a stout stick with strong twine, and filing off
the barb. Always clean your gaff after a day's fishing
with emery paper. and apply a little vaseline.

F

3. CLOTHING.—Wear the oldest clothes for sea-fishing with coloured flannel shirt, and in cold weather wrap up warmly. A blue-knitted " guernsey," such as fishermen wear, will be found a great comfort in keeping the body warm. A waterproof apron is useful in protecting the clothes from wet in hauling lines and gear. For keeping the feet warm and dry there is nothing equal to a pair of long waterproof boots, with a pair of thick stockings underneath. The best boots are made of leather, covered with rubber, and a pair will last for years. If raining, pull your trousers over them, so that the water will not enter the boots. To dry the inside, heat some beans in the oven and pour them into the boots, leaving them all night. In the morning they will be found quite dry and ready to wear.

4. Always steep your gut-tackle in fresh water for a few minutes after use. Also spread your hand-line to dry on a grass-plot, or any convenient spot, before you wind it on the frame. Remove artificial baits from the line; rinse them in fresh water, and dry carefully; this will prevent their tarnishing. Polish spinners with a little plate-powder and a brush, and always use them as bright as possible.

5. Never purchase small hooks, gut, snooding, or lines in any but the very best shops.

6. Do not use bait that is in the least tainted, except on certain occasions which have been mentioned.

7. Never go out without knife, gaff, and plenty of spare tackle, sinkers, and hooks, in case of emergency.

8. When whiffing alone, always attach the oars securely to the gunwale by short lanyards in case you should drop one overboard.

9. When going out on a night-fishing expedition, never take with you a nervous, fidgety companion. Never go out without plenty of matches, and at least four lanterns—one for mast-head, one for stern, one for bow, and one for use when baiting, unhooking, &c. The lantern on mast-head (pole fastened to centre seat, and

about 7ft. high) should have red glass; the common stable lanterns are the best.

10. If the night is cold, remember that hot coffee is the most warming of all fluids. You can bring it ready-made in a covered can, and re-heat it over a spirit or an oil lamp arrangement. But vacuum flasks avoid all this trouble, as tea, cocoa, coffee, or soup may be kept hot for twenty-four hours. The heat engendered in the system by coffee lasts many times as long as the heat caused by ardent spirits. Once September comes in, the nights are invariably cold at sea.

11. Never argue on politics or religion with your boatman. Carry an old watch with you to which a leather or hair chain is attached.

12. See that all your gear is in good order before you start. Use fine but strong lines adapted to the fish you are seeking, and, guided by the foregoing instructions, you cannot fail to enjoy some success in sea-fishing.

CHAPTER XII.

FISHING STATIONS.

TO those fond of sea-fishing, I think the following particulars of various English and Welsh fishing-stations will be of use, as it will enable them to select the place best calculated to give good results at the time of the year they are able to get away. The list has been compiled from particulars supplied by residents in the places mentioned, and every care has been taken to insure accuracy; but it is needless to say that I should be greatly indebted to any readers who will point out any errors, or supply additional information for use in a future edition.

Aberayron (Cardiganshire).—*Fishing* : Good. *Fish* : Bass, cod, gurnard, mackerel, &c. *Best Months* : March to September.

Aberdovey (Merionethshire).—*Fishing* : Good. *Fish* : Bass, codling, flat fish, mackerel, sewin, pollack, &c. *Best Months* : June to October.

Aberporth (Cardiganshire).—*Fishing* : Fair. *Fish* : Ground-fish and bass. *Best Months* : June to October.

Aberystwyth (Cardiganshire). — *Fishing* : Good. *Fish* : Bass, gurnard, herring, mackerel, skate, &c. *Best Months* : August to October.

Aldeburgh (Suffolk).—*Fishing* : Good. *Fish* : Bass, cod, codling, eel, sole, plaice, whiting, &c. *Best Months* : June to November.

Alderney.—*Fishing* : Very good. *Fish* : Atherine, bass, bream, conger, garfish, mackerel, pollack, whiting, &c. *Best Months* : April to July.

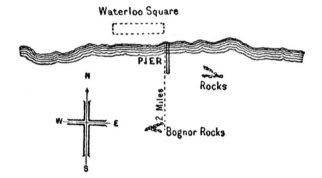

Fig. 56.—Chart of the Bognor Fishing-grounds, showing positions of rocks.

Allonby (Cumberland).—*Fishing* : Fair. *Fish* : Codling, flounder, herring, sole, &c. *Best Months* : June to October.

Alnmouth (Northumberland).—*Fishing* : Good. *Fish* : Flounder, gurnard, flat-fish, haddock, mackerel, saithe, whiting, &c. *Best Months* : June to September.

Appledore (N. Devon).—*Fishing* : Fair. *Fish* : Bass. *Best Months* : June to September.

Bamburgh (Northumberland).—*Fishing* : Good. *Fish* : Billet, cod, flat-fish, haddock, ling, lythe, mackerel, &c. *Best Months* : June to September.

Bantham (S. Devon).—*Fishing* : Good. *Fish* : Bass, pilchards, pollack, &c. *Best Months* : June to September.

Barmouth (Merionethshire).—*Fishing* : Good. *Fish* : Bass, codling, haddock, mackerel, pollack, skate, whiting, &c. *Best Months* : August to October.

Beaumaris (Anglesey).—*Fishing* : Very good. *Fish* : Bass, cod, codling, gurnard, herring, mackerel, mullet, pollack, sole, turbot, whitebait, whiting, &c. *Best Months* : July to October

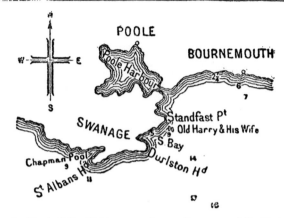

Fig. 57.—Chart of the Fishing-grounds near Swanage and Bournemouth, with depth in fathoms.

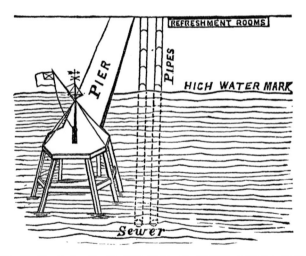

Fig. 58.—Chart showing Position of Sewage Outfall at Bournemouth— a good station for flat fish, whiting, and chad.

Bembridge (I. of Wight).—*Fishing* : Fair. *Fish* : Herring, mackerel whiting, pout, &c. *Best Months* : June to September. A chart of the Isle of Wight is given in Fig 68.

Bexhill (Sussex).—*Fishing* : Poor. *Fish* : Bream, cod, eel, plaice, whiting &c. *Best Months* : April to September. The coast eastwards to Rye Bay and westwards to Beachy Head is shown in the chart, Fig. 63.

Bideford (N. Devon).—*Fishing* : Fair. *Fish* : Bass. *Best Months* : June to October.

Blackpool (Lancs.).—*Fishing* : Fair. *Fish* : Codling, mackerel, and flat-fish *Best Months* : June to October.

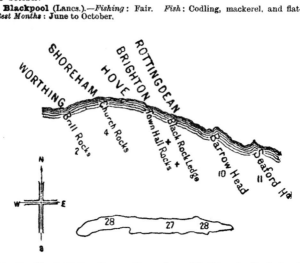

Fig. 59.—Chart of the Sussex Coast from Worthing to Seaford. The crosses show the best spots and the figures the depth in fathoms.

Bognor (Sussex).—*Fishing* : Good. *Fish* : Bass, black bream, cod, flat-fish, mackerel, whiting, wrasse, &c. *Best Months* : August to October. The fishing grounds are shown in the chart, Fig. 56, and the adjacent coast in Fig 60.

Bonchurch (I. of Wight).—*Fishing* : Fair *Best Months* : June to September.

Boscastle (Cornwall).—*Fishing* : Fair. *Fish* : Flat-fish, mackerel, pollack, &c. *Best Months* ; July to October.

Bournemouth (Hants).—*Fishing* : Fair. *Fish* : Chad, dab, flat-fish, smelt and whiting. *Best Months* : August to October. A chart of the Bournemouth, Poole, and Swanage stations is given in Fig. 57, and Fig. 58 shows the position of the sewage outfall—an excellent spot for flat-fish, whiting, and chad, and by no means offensive.

Bridlington Quay (Yorks.).—*Fishing* : Good. *Fish* : Billet, brill, cod, codling, dab, eel, gurnard, herring, mackerel, plaice, pollack, sole, turbot whiting, &c. *Best Months* : July to October.

Bridport (Dorset).—*Fishing :* Fair. *Fish :* Bass, blinn, bream, conger mackerel, grey mullet, pollack, pout, &c. *Best Months :* June to September.

Brightlingsea (Essex).—*Fishing :* Fair. *Fish :* Codling, plaice, whiting &c. *Best Months :* September and October.

Brighton (Sussex).—*Fishing :* Fair. *Fish :* Bass, bream, cod, conger, plaice, pollack, whiting, &c. *Best Months :* July to November. The best spots are shown by the crosses in the chart, Fig. 59; and the larger chart (Fig. 60) indicates a favourite ground.

Brixham (S. Devon).—*Fishing :* Very good. *Fish :* Bass, bream, conger dab, mackerel, plaice, pollack, whiting, &c. *Best Months :* July to October.

Broad Haven (Pemb.).—*See* Little Haven.

Broadstairs (Kent).—*Fishing:* Very fair. *Fish :* Cod, codling, bass, conger, dab, plaice, and whiting-pout. *Best Months :* August to October. A chart of the neighbouring coast is given in Fig. 71.

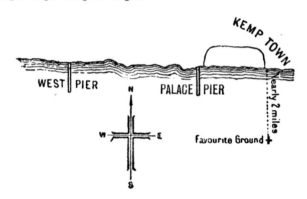

Fig. 6o.—Chart showing a favourite Fishing-ground about 2 miles off Kemp Town, Brighton.

Bude (Cornwall).—*Fishing :* Fair. *Fish :* Bass, grey mullet, &c. *Best Months :* June to October.

Budleigh Salterton (S. Devon).—*Fishing :* Good. *Fish :* Bass, conger, dab, mackerel, grey mullet, pollack, pout, rock-fish, whiting. *Best Months :* July to October. A chart of the coast in this district is given in Fig. 61.

Burnham (Som.).—*Fishing :* Fair. *Fish :* Cod, dab, flounder, plaice, sole, &c. *Best Months :* May to December.

Carnarvon.—*Fishing :* Good. *Fish :* Bass, gurnard, and mackerel. *Best Months :* July to September.

Charmouth (Dorset).—*Fishing :* Fair. *Fish :* Rock-whiting, &c. *Best Months :* May to September.

Christchurch (Hants.).—*Fishing :* Good. *Fish :* Bass, mackerel, pollack. *Best Months :* June to August. The position of Christchurch Ledge is indicated in the chart of the Isle of Wight (Fig. 68).

Clacton-on-Sea (Essex).—*Fishing* : Poor. *Fish* : Plaice, whiting, &c. *Best Months* : September and October

Cleethorpes (Lincs.).—*Fishing* : Fair. *Fish* : Cod, conger, haddock, ling, plaice, skate, sole. &c. *Best Months* : June to October.

Clevedon (Som.).—*Fishing* : Fair. *Fish* : Cod, conger, dab, sole, whiting, &c. *Best Months* : July to November.

Clovelly (N. Devon).—*Fishing* : Good. *Fish* : Bass, skate, conger, bream, &c. *Best Months* : June to October.

Colwyn Bay (Denbighshire).—*Fishing* : Fair. *Fish* : Bass and flat-fish. *Best Months* : July to October.

Combe Martin (N. Devon).—*Fishing* Fair. *Fish* : Bream, cod, pollack &c. *Best Months* : June to October. The coast from here to Morte Bay is shown in Fig. 67.

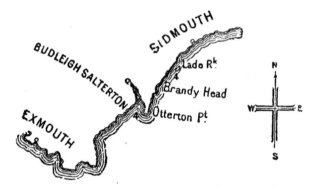

Fig. 61.—Chart of the South Devon Coast from Exmouth to Sidmouth, showing the depth in fathoms. Budleigh Salterton is a very good station.

Cowes (I. of Wight).—*Fishing* : Fair. *Fish* : Bass, mackerel, mullet, smelt, &c. *Best Months* : July to October. A chart of the Isle of Wight is given in Fig. 68.

Criccieth (Carnarvonshire).—*Fishing* : Fair. *Fish* : Flounder, gurnard skate, whiting, &c. *Best Months* : June to September.

Cromer (Norfolk).—*Fishing* : Fair. *Fish* : Bass, codling, mackerel, plaice, and whiting. *Best Months* : July to October.

Dartmouth (S. Devon).—*Fishing* : Fair. *Fish* : Bass, conger, pollack, whiting. *Best Month* : August.

Dawlish (S. Devon).—*Fishing* : Good. *Fish* : Dab, herring, mackerel, whiting-pollack, whiting-pout, and whiting. *Best Months* : March to September.

Deal (Kent).—*Fishing* : Very good. *Fish* : Cod, codling, dab, horse-mackerel, plaice, pollack, pout, whiting, &c. *Best Months* : July, October to January. A favourite fishing ground is shown in Fig. 62. and Figs 71 and 74 are charts of the adjacent coast.

Devonport (S. Devon).—*Fishing* : Good. *Fish* : Bass, chad, grey mullet, mackerel, pollack, smelt, &c. *Best Months* : May to November. A chart of Plymouth Sound is shown in Fig. 73.

Dinas Dinlle (Carnarvonshire).—*Fishing* : Fair. *Fish* : Bass, flat-fish, mackerel, &c. *Best Months* : June to October.

Douglas (I. of Man).—*Fishing* : Good. *Fish* : Cod, conger, fluke, herring, mackerel, pollack, whiting, &c. *Best Months* : June to September

Dover (Kent).—*Fishing* : Good. *Fish* : Bass, codling, flounders, mackerel, mullet, pollack, rock-fish, smelt, whiting-pout, &c. *Best Months* : June to September.

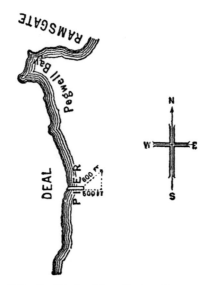

Fig. 62.—Chart of the Kentish Coast from Deal to Ramsgate. The cross shows a favourite fishing-ground near the pier.

Dovercourt (Essex).—*Fishing* : Poor. *Fish* : Codling, mullet, and sole. *Best Months* : March to November.

Downderry (Cornwall).—*Fishing* : Good. *Fish* : Pollack, &c. *Best Months* : July to October.

Eastbourne (Sussex).—*Fishing* : Fair. *Fish* : Bass, bream, cod, conger, dab, plaice, pollack, sole, whiting, &c. *Best Months* : August to October. The coast from here to Rye Bay is shown in the chart, Fig. 63.

Exmouth (S. Devon).—*Fishing* : Good. *Fish* : Bass, bream, conger, dab, eel, flounder, mackerel, plaice, pollack, whiting, &c. *Best Months* : May to October. A chart of the coast from here to Sidmouth is given in Fig. 61.

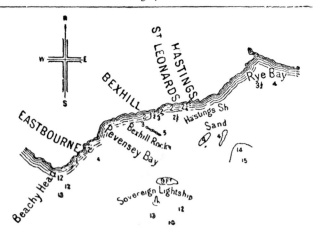

Fig. 63.—Chart of the Sussex Coast from Beachy Head to Rye Bay, showing depth in fathoms. Hastings Pier is one of the best spots for pout.

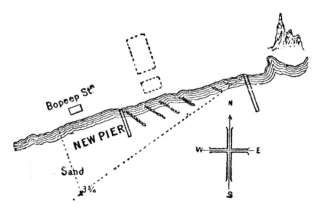

Fig. 64.—Chart showing a favourite ground off Bopeep Station, Hastings, with the depth in fathoms. The New Pier is a good place for whiting, bass, and conger.

Falmouth (Cornwall).—*Fishing* : Good. *Fish* : Bass, chad, cod, conger, gurnard, hake, mackerel, grey mullet, pollack, &c. *Best Months* : July to October.

Felixstowe (Suffolk).—*Fishing* : Fair. *Fish* : Plaice, sole, whiting, &c. *Best Months* : September and October.

Ferryside (Carmarthenshire).—*Fishing* : Fair. *Fish* : Bass, mackerel, &c. *Best Months* : June to October.

Filey (Yorks.).—*Fishing* : Very good. *Fish* : Brill, coalfish, cod, conger, dab, gurnard, haddock, parr, plaice, pollack, and whiting. *Best Months* : June to September. A chart of the coast from here to Scarborough is given in Fig. 75, the best grounds being indicated by crosses.

Fishguard (Pemb.)—*Fishing* : Good. *Fish* : Codling, conger, crab, gurnard, ling, lobster, mackerel, plaice, pollack, and whiting. *Best Months* : July to September.

Flamborough (Yorks.).—*Fishing* : Good. *Fish* : Billet, coalfish, pollack, &c. *Best Months* : June to October.

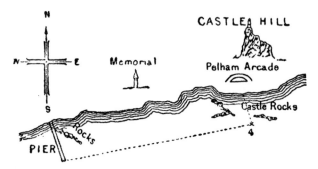

Fig. 65.—Chart of the Hastings Coast from the New Pier to a good swim off the Castle Rocks, with depth in fathoms.

Fleetwood (Lancs.).—*Fishing* : Poor. *Fish* : Brill, cod, gurnard, sole, whiting, &c. *Best Months* : May to January.

Folkestone (Kent).—*Fishing* : Very good. *Fish* : Bass, cod, plaice, sole, and whiting. *Best Months* : July to October.

Fowey (Cornwall).—*Fishing* : Very good. *Fish* : Cod, conger, ling, mackerel, gurnard, plaice, pollack, sole, whiting, &c. *Best Months* : July to October.

Freshwater (I. of Wight).—*Fishing* : Fair. *Fish* : Bass, mullet, and whiting. *Best Months* : June and July for whiting; winter months for the rest.

Goodwick (Pemb.).—*Fishing* : Poor. *Fish* : Mackerel, plaice, whiting, &c. *Best Months* : August and September.

Grimsby (Lincs.).—*Fishing* : Fair. *Fish* : Codling, conger, flounder, smelt, whiting, &c. *Best Months* : June to September.

Guernsey.—*Fishing* . Good. *Fish* : Bass, brill, cod, conger, dory, gurnard, mackerel, mullet, plaice, pollack, ray, sole, turbot, rock-fish, whiting, &c. *Best Months* : June to September.

Gwbert (Cardiganshire).—*Fishing* : Fair. *Best Months* : June to October.

Hartland (N. Devon).—*Fishing* : Good. *Fish* : Bass. *Best Months* : June to October

Harwich (Essex).—*Fishing* : Fair. *Fish* : Cod, conger, whiting, &c. *Best Months* : May to October.

Hastings (Sussex).—*Fishing* : Good. *Fish* : Bass, bream, conger, gurnard, pollack, sole, whiting-pout, &c. *Best Months* : June to October. The coast from Beachy Head to Rye Bay is shown in the chart, Fig. 63. The crosses in Figs. 64 to 66 indicate some favourite grounds off Bo-Peep Station, the Castle Rocks, and the rocks opposite Warrior Square respectively.

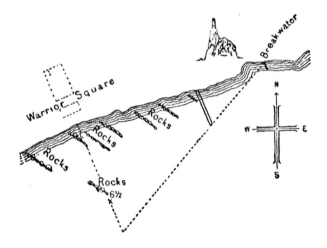

Fig. 66.—Chart showing a capital ground (×) oft the Rocks near Warrior Square, Hastings, with depth in fathoms.

Hayling Island (Hants.).—*Fishing* : Good. *Fish* : Bass, mackerel, grey and red mullet, plaice, rock-fish, sole, whiting, &c. *Best Months* : June to August.

Herne Bay (Kent).—*Fishing* : Good. *Fish* : Tope, bass, dab, plaice, pout, sole, whiting, &c. *Best Months* : May to September.

Holkham (Norfolk).—*Fishing*. Good. *Fish* : Brill, butt, cod, mackerel, mullet, salmon, trout, plaice, &c. *Best Months* : March to October.

Holyhead (Anglesey).—*Fishing* : Good. *Fish* : Pollack, whiting, bream, conger, &c. *Best Months* : August to October.

Hornsea (Yorks.).—*Fishing* : Fair. *Fish* : Cod, ling, mackerel, and whiting. *Best Months* : June to September.

Hoylake (Cheshire).—*Fishing* : Poor. *Fish* : Flounders, whiting, and codling.

Hunstanton (Norfolk).—*Fishing* : Poor. *Fish* : Flat-fish. *Best Months* : March to October.

Hythe (Kent).—*Fishing* : Good. *Fish* : Bass, cod mackerel, plaice, sole and whiting. *Best Months* : July to October.

Ilfracombe (N. Devon).—*Fishing* : Good. *Fish* : Bass, bream, cod, conger. flat-fish, ling, mullet, pollack, tamlin, whiting, &c. *Best Months* : August, October, and December. A chart of the adjacent coast is given in Fig. 67.

Instow (N. Devon).—*Fishing* : Good. *Fish* : Bass, cod, salmon. *Best Months* : May to October.

Isle of Man.—Particulars of the fishing-grounds are given under Douglas Port Erin, and Ramsey.

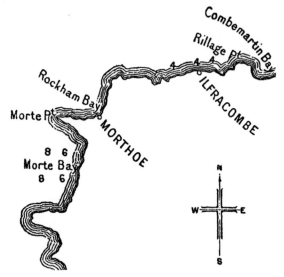

Fig. 67.—Chart of the North Devon Coast from Morte Bay to Combe Martin Bay, with depth in fathoms. Very large ling and conger are taken off Ilfracombe.

Isle of Wight.—The east coast of the island affords the best fishing. Particulars are given under Bembridge, Cowes, Ryde, Sandown, Totland Bay. and Ventnor. A chart of the island is shown in Fig. 68.

Jersey.—*Fishing* : Good. *Fish* : Bass, bream, conger, mackerel, mullet. plaice, pollack, pout, rock-fish, sole, whiting. *Best Months* : April to July.

Kingsbridge (S. Devon).—*Fishing* : Good *Fish* : Bass, &c. *Best Months* : June to October.

Kingsdown (Kent).—*Fishing* : Fair. *Best Months* : June to October.

Lancing (Sussex).—*Fishing* · Fair. *Best Months* : June to September.

Fig. 68.—Chart of the Isle of Wight, showing depth in fathoms. The best fishing-grounds are on the east coast, from Ryde to Sandown. Christchurch Ledge and the Outer Nab are good spots.

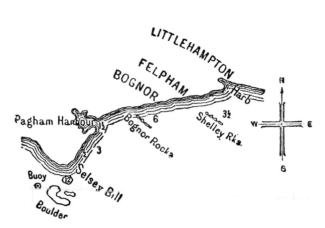

Fig. 69.—Chart of the Sussex Coast from Selsey Bill to Littlehampton, shewing depth in fathoms. Littlehampton Harbour is a fine spot for bass and grey mullet. An enlarged chart of the Bognor station is given in Fig. 56.

Lee (N. Devon).—*Fishing* : Good. *Fish* : Bass, cod, pollack, whiting, &c. *Best Months* : June to August.

Lee-on-Solent (Hants.).—*Fishing* : Poor *Fish* : Whiting, bass, &c. *Best Months* : September and October.

Littlehampton (Sussex).—*Fishing* : Fair. *Fish* : Bass, bream, eel, grey mullet, and smelt. *Best Months* : May and June. A chart of the adjacent coast is given in Fig. 69.

Little Haven and Broad Haven (Pemb.).—*Fishing* : Fair. *Fish* : bass mackerel, pollack, &c. *Best Months* : June to September.

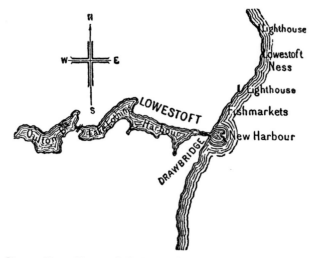

Fig. 70.—Chart of Lowestoft Harbour and the adjacent coast. The harbour abounds in smelts and eels, and the shore in codling.

Lizard (Cornwall).—*Fishing* : Good. *Fish* : Bass, pollack, &c. *Best Months* : June to October.

Llandudno (Carnarvonshire).—*Fishing* : Good. *Fish* : Codling, conger, pollack, crab, dab, flounder, whiting, &c. *Best Months* : June to September.

Llanfairfechan (Carnarvonshire).—*Fishing* : Fair. *Fish* : Bass, codling dab, mackerel, mullet, plaice, sole, &c. *Best Months* : April to October.

Llangranog (Cardiganshire).—*Fishing* : Good. *Fish* : Bass, cod, gurnet mackerel, sewin, sole, and whiting. *Best Months* : July to November.

Llanstephan (Carmarthenshire).—*Fishing* : Fair. *Fish* : Sewin, &c. *Best Months* : July and August.

Looe, East and West (Cornwall).—*Fishing* : Good. *Fish* : Bass, chad, mackerel, pollack, ray, skate, whiting, &c. *Best Months* : August to November

Lowestoft (Suffolk).—*Fishing* : Good. *Fish* : Butt, codling, conger mackerel, mullet, plaice, smelt, whiting, &c. *Best Months* : August to October A chart of the harbour and coast is given in Fig. 70.

Lyme Regis (Dorset).—*Fishing* : Fair. *Fish* : Bass, mackerel, &c. *Best Months* : June to September.

Lymington (Hants).—*Fishing* : Fair. *Fish* : Bass, flounder, grey mullet, plaice, &c. *Best Months* : June to September.

Lynmouth (N. Devon).—*Fishing* : Fairly good. *Fish* : Bass, conger, eel, mackerel, grey mullet, pollack, rock-fish, whiting, &c. *Best Months* : May to September.

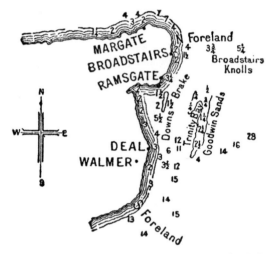

Fig. 71.—Chart of the Kentish Coast from Margate to the South Foreland, giving the depth in fathoms. An enlarged chart of the Ramsgate and Pegwell Bay district is given in Fig. 74, and another of Ramsgate to Deal in Fig. 62.

Lytham (Lancs.).—*Fishing* : Fair. *Fish* : Codling, fluke, gurnard, mackerel, ray, sole, skate, turbot, &c. *Best Months* : July to September.

Mablethorpe (Lincs.).—*Fish* : Sole, plaice, &c.

Maldon (Essex).—*Fishing* : Fair. *Fish* : Cod, dab, ling, whiting, &c. *Best Months* : June to November.

Manorbier (Pemb.).—*Fishing* : Fair. *Fish* : Bass, gurnard, grey and red mullet, plaice, &c. *Best Months* : May to September. A chart of the coast from here to Tenby is given in Fig. 78.

Marazion (Cornwall).—*Fishing* : Good. *Fish* : Bream, chad, conger, hake, mackerel whiting, &c. *Best Months* : July to October.

Margate (Kent).—*Fishing*: Very good. *Fish*: Bass, tope, conger, flounder, mackerel, mullet, pollack, and whiting. *Best Months*: August to October. A chart of the coast from Margate to the South Foreland is given in Fig. 71, and another of Ramsgate and district in Fig. 74.

Marske (Yorks.).—*Fishing*: Fair. *Fish*: Cod, dab, codling, flat-fish, gurnard, haddock, whiting, &c. *Best Months*: May to September.

Mevagissey (Cornwall).—*Fishing*: Good. *Fish*: Bass, bream, chad, cod, conger, dab, gurnard, herring, mackerel, ling, pilchard, pollack, &c. *Best Months*: March to September. A chart of the coast from here to Dodman Point is given in Fig. 72.

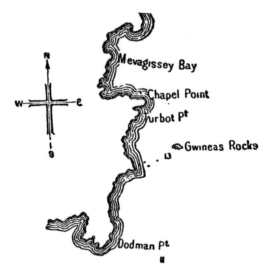

Fig. 72.—Chart of the South Cornish Coast from Mevagissey Bay to Dodman Point, showing the depth in fathoms. Fishing can be had in the bay all the year round.

Milford Haven (Pemb.).—*Fishing*: Good. *Fish*: Cod, gurnard, flat-fish, and whiting. *Best Months*: June to November.

Minehead (Som.).—*Fishing*: Poor. *Fish*: Dab, whiting, &c. *Best Months*: July to October.

Morecambe Bay (Lancs.).—*Fishing*: Good. *Fish*: Codling, conger, fluke, and flat-fish. *Best Months*: August and September.

Mudeford (Hants.).—*Fishing*: Good. *Fish*: Bass, mackerel, pollack, whiting-pout, and whiting. *Best Months*: May to October.

Mullion (Cornwall).—*Fishing*: Good. *Fish*: Conger, pollack, bream, bass, &c. *Best Months*: June to October.

G

Mumbles (Glam.).—*Fishing*: Poor. *Fish*: Whiting, conger, cod, &c.

New Brighton (Cheshire).—*Fishing*: Poor. *Fish*: Whiting. *Best Months* ı March and April.

Newhaven (Sussex).—*Fishing*: Good. *Fish*: Bass, whiting, &c. *Best Months*: June to October.

Newport (Pemb.).—*Fishing*: Good. *Fish*: Bass, gurnard, mackerel, pollack whiting, &c. *Best Months* : June to September.

New Quay (Cardiganshire).—*Fishing*: Good. *Fish*: Pollack, bass, haddock, mackerel, sole, turbot, and whiting. *Best Months* : June to August.

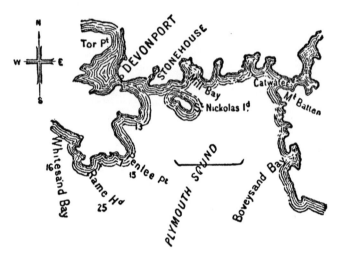

Fig. 73.—Chart of Plymouth Sound, showing the depth in fathoms. A very fine station. Most fish can be taken here.

Newquay (Cornwall).—*Fishing*: Fair. *Fish* : Bream, mackerel, pollack, mullet, bass, sole, &c. *Best Months* : June to October.

Padstow (Cornwall).—*Fishing*: Good. *Fish*: Bass, conger, gurnard, mackerel, mullet, plaice, pollack, skate, smelt, turbot, &c. *Best Months*: June to August.

Paignton (S. Devon).—*Fishing*: Fair. *Fish*: Bass, conger, dab, mackerel, pollack, whiting, &c. *Best Months*: May to October. A chart of Torbay is shown in Fig. 79.

Palling (Norfolk).—*Fishing*: Fair. *Fish*: Mackerel, plaice, sole, &c. *Best Months*: March to October.

Par (Cornwall).—*Fishing*: Fair. *Fish*: Conger, pollack, &c. *Best Months* : June to September.

Parkstone (Dorset).—*Fishing* : Fair. *Fish* : Bass, conger, dab, grey mullet, pollack, whiting, wrasse.

Peel (I. of Man).—*Fishing* : Very good. *Fish* : Bream, cod, codling, conger, flat-fish, gurnard, mackerel, plaice, pollack, rock-cod, whiting, wrasse, &c. *Best Months* : June to August.

Pembrey and Burry Port (Carmarthenshire).—*Fishing* : Fair. *Fish* : Bass, cod, conger, gurnard, mackerel, mullet, &c. *Best Months* : May to August.

Pendine (Carmarthenshire).—*Fishing* : Fair. *Fish* : Bret, plaice, sewin, sole, &c. *Best Months* : May to August.

Penmaenmawr (Carnarvonshire).—*Fishing* : Good. *Fish* : Bass, cod, &c. *Best Months* : June to October.

Penzance (Cornwall).—*Fishing* : Very good. *Fish* : Bream, chad, cod, conger, gurnard, hake, mackerel, mullet, pollack, and whiting. *Best Months* : July to September.

Plymouth (S. Devon).—*Fishing* : Excellent. *Fish* : Bass, bream, chad, cod, conger, dory, gurnard, hake mackerel, mullet, pollack, smelt, whiting, &c. *Best Months* : June to October. A chart of the Sound is shown in Fig. 73.

Polperro (Cornwall).—*Fishing* : Good. *Fish* : Bream, conger, mackerel, pollack, whiting. *Best Months* : June to October.

Poole (Dorset).—*Fishing* : Poor. *Fish* : Codling, conger, pollack, smelt, whiting, &c. *Best Months* : July to November. A chart of Poole Harbour and adjacent coast is given in Fig. 57.

Port Erin (I. of Man).—*Fishing* : Very good. *Fish* : Cod, codling, conger, gurnard, mackerel, plaice, pollack, whiting, &c. *Best Months* : August and September.

Porthcawl (Glam.).—*Fishing* : Fair. *Fish* : Bass, mackerel, &c. *Best Months* : June to September.

Portscatho (Cornwall).—*Fishing* : Good. *Fish* : Bass, bream, pollack, &c. *Best Months* : May to September.

Prussia Cove (Cornwall).—*Fishing* : Good. *Fish* : Cod, conger, hake, and pollack. *Best Months* : April to October.

Pwllheli (Carnarvonshire).—*Fishing* : Fair. *Fish* : Bass, brill, codling, gurnard, plaice, skate, sole, turbot, whiting, &c. *Best Months* : April to September.

Ramsey (I. of Man).—*Fishing* : Good. *Fish* : Bream, coalfish, cod, codling, conger, fluke, herring, ling, mackerel, plaice, pollack, whiting, wrasse, &c. *Best Months* : April to September.

Ramsgate (Kent).—*Fishing* : Fair. *Fish* : Bass, brill, cod, codling, dab, flat-fish, flounder, mullet, plaice, sole, and whiting. *Best Months* : July to October. Fig. 62 shows a chart of the coast from here to Deal; Fig. 71 from Margate to the South Foreland; and Fig. 74 of Ramsgate and Pegwell Bay.

Redcar (Yorks.).—*Fishing* : Very good. *Fish* : Codling, dab, haddock, mackerel, whiting, &c. *Best Months* : May to September.

Roker.—*Fishing* : Fair. *Fish* : Billet, cod, codling, conger, dab, gurnard, haddock, halibut, mackerel, rockling, skate, sole, whiting, &c. *Best Months* : May to September.

Runswick.—*Fishing* : Fair. *Fish* : Cod, ling, haddock, &c. *Best Months* : June to November.

Ryde (I. of Wight).—*Fishing* : Good. *Fish* : Bass, mackerel, pollack, whiting-pout, &c. *Best Months* : July to September. A chart of the Isle of Wight is given in Fig. 68.

Rye (Kent). - *Fishing* : Fair. *Fish* : Bass, flat-fish, &c. A chart of the coast from here to Beachy Head is given in Fig. 68.

St. An'e's (Lancs.).—*Fishing* : Poor. *Fish* : Flat-fish, &c.

G *

St. Bees (Cumberland).—*Fishing* : Fair. *Fish* : Cod. *Best Months* : February, March, September, and October.

St. David's (Pemb.).—*Fishing* : Good. *Fish* : Coal-fish, pollack, bream, bass, &c. *Best Months* : July to September.

St. Ives (Cornwall).—*Fishing* : Good. *Fish* : Bass, bream, cod, conger, gurnard, hake, ling, plaice, pollack, skate, &c. *Best Months* : May to October.

St. Leonards (Sussex).—*Fishing* : Good. *Fish* : Bream, conger, gurnard, sole, whiting, &c. *Best Months* : June to October. A chart of the coast east and west of St. Leonards is given in Fig. 63.

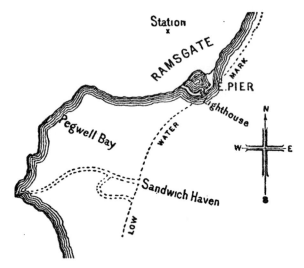

Fig. 74.—Chart of Ramsgate, Pegwell Bay, and Sandwich Haven. The adjacent coasts are shown in Figs. 62 and 71.

St. Margaret's Bay (Kent).—*Fish* : Mackerel, whiting, &c. *Best Months* : May to October.

St. Mawes (Cornwall).—*Fishing* : Good. *Fish* : Bass, chad, conger mackerel, pollack, &c. *Best Months* : May to September.

Salcombe (S. Devon).—*Fishing* : Good. *Fish* : Bass, chad, mackerel, &c. *Best Months* : July to September.

Saltburn (Yorks.).—*Fishing* : Good. *Fish* : Billet, cod, codling, conger, flat-fish, gurnard, haddock, ling, mackerel, whiting, &c. *Best Months* : June to September.

Sandgate (Kent).—*Fishing* : Good. *Fish* : Bass, brill, cod, conger, dab, flounders, mackerel, plaice, sole, whiting, &c. *Best Months* : May to October

Sandown (I. of Wight).—*Fishing* : Good.   **Fish** : Bass, bream conger, mackerel, gurnard, pollack, whiting-pout, wrasse, &c.   *Best Months* : May to September.   A chart of the Isle of Wight is given in Fig. 68.

Sandwich (Kent).—*Fishing* : Fair.   **Fish** : Bass, codling, dab, grey mullet, plaice.   *Best Months* : May to October.   A chart of Sandwich Haven, Ramsgate, and Pegwell Bay is given in Fig. 74.

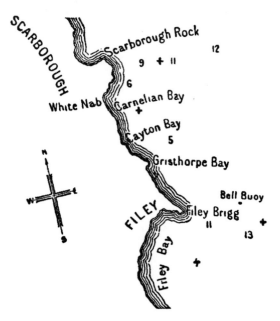

Fig. 75.—Chart of the Yorkshire Coast from Scarborough to Filey Bay. The crosses indicate the best stations and the figures the depth in fathoms.   Scarborough is an excellent fishing-station.

Sark.—*Fishing* : Good.   **Fish** : Bass, conger, mackerel, pollack, whiting, &c. *Best Months* : April to July.

Saundersfoot (Pemb.).—*Fishing* : Good   **Fish** : Bass, cod, gurnard, mackerel, plaice, pollack, sewin, sole, whiting, &c.   *Best Months* : July to September.

Scarborough (Yorks.).—*Fishing* : Excellent.   **Fish** : Bass, billet, cod, coalfish, codling, conger, dab, gurnard, haddock, mackerel, plaice, pollack, whiting, &c.   *Best Months* : July to September.   A chart of the coast from here to Filey Bay is given in Fig. 75, the best grounds being indicated by crosses.

Scilly Isles.—*Fishing* : Very good. *Fish* : Bream, chad, cod, conger, hake ling, mullet, pollack, ray, rock-cod, skate, turbot, &c. *Best Months* : May to November.

Seaford (Sussex).—*Fishing* : Fair. *Fish* : Rock-pout, whiting, &c. Better fishing-grounds are at Brighton, as indicated by the crosses in Fig. 59.

Seaham Harbour (Durham).—*Fishing* : Fair. *Fish* : Codling, gurnard, haddock, mackerel, sole, whiting, &c. *Best Months* : June to September.

Seaton (S. Devon).—*Fishing* : Good. *Fish* : Bass, mackerel, pollack, pout, whiting. *Best Months* : May to September.

Seaton Carew (Durham).—*Fishing* : Good. *Fish* : Dab, gurnard, haddock. plaice, sole, whiting, &c. *Best Months* : June to September.

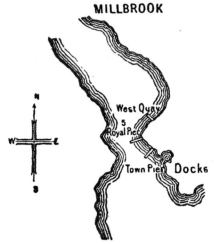

Fig. 76.—Chart of Southampton Water, showing depth in fathoms near the Royal Pier—a good station for mullet.

Sea View (I. of Wight).—*Fishing* : Fair. *Fish* : Bass, herring, mackerel. &c. *Best Months* : July to September.

Selsey (Hants).—*Fishing* : Fair. *Fish* : Bass, bream, mackerel, mullet, pollack, smelt, &c. *Best Months* : June to September. The coast from Selsea Bill to Littlehampton Harbour is shown in Fig 69.

Sheringham (Norfolk).—*Fishing* : Good. *Fish* : Bass, codling, gurnard, mackerel, &c. *Best Months* : August and September.

Shoreham (Sussex).—*Fishing* : Fair. *Fish* : Bass, bream, dab, mackerel, plaice, pollack, pout, whiting. *Best Months* : May to October. The chart, Fig. 59, shows the coast from here to Seaford.

Sidmouth (S. Devon).—*Fishing* : Good. *Fish* : Bass, mackerel, pollack, pout, and whiting. *Best Months* : August and September. A chart of the coast from Exmouth to Sidmouth is given in Fig. 61.

Silloth (Cumberland).—*Fishing* : Good. *Fish* : Codling (winter); plaice. sole, &c. (summer).

Silverdale (Lancs.).—*Fishing* : Fair. *Fish* : Flat-fish, &c. *Best Months* : June to August.

Skegness (Lincs.).—*Fishing* : Poor. *Fish* : Plaice, sole, &c. *Best Months* : May to July.

Skinburness (Cumberland).—*Fishing* : Fair.

Slapton (S. Devon).—*Fishing* : Very good. *Fish* : Bass, mullet, pollack. whiting, &c. *Best Months* : June to October.

Solva (Pemb.).—*Fishing* : Fair. *Fish* : Gurnard, mackerel, whiting, &c.

Fig. 77.—Chart of the Estuaries of the Thames and Medway, showing the depth in fathoms. There are swarms of dabs off Southend.

Southampton (Hants.).—*Fishing* : Good. *Fish* : Bass, eel, flat-fish, grey mullet, pout, whiting. *Best Months* : April and May. A chart of Southampton Water is shown in Fig 76.

Southbourne (Hants.).—*Fishing* : Fair. *Fish* : Mackerel, sole, whiting, &c. *Best Months* : May to September.

Southend (Essex).—*Fishing* : Poor. *Fish* : Dab, flounder, plaice. *Best Months* : October to February. A chart of the estuary of the Thames is given in Fig. 77.

Southport (Lancs.).—*Fishing* : Fair. *Fish* : Whiting, codling, and flat-fish. *Best Months* : July to September.

Southsea (Hants).—*Fishing* : Poor. *Fish* : Bass, conger, mackerel, whiting, &c. *Best Months* : July to September.

South Shields (Durham).—*Fishing* : Good. *Fish* : Cod, codling, eel, flounder, fluke, gurnard, haddock, herring, mackerel, whiting, &c. *Best Months* : Middle of July to end of October.

Southwold (Suffolk).—*Fishing* : Fair. *Fish* : Cod, codling, eel, flounder, plaice, skate, whiting, &c. *Best Months* : September and October.

Spittal (Northumberland).—*Fish* : Gurnard, rock-cod, whiting. *Best Months* : April to October.

Sutton-on-Sea (Lincs.).—*Fishing* : Fair. *Fish* : Cod, skate, sole, &c. *Best Months* : May to September.

Swanage (Dorset).—*Fishing* : Fair. *Fish* : Bass, conger, flat-fish. mullet, pollack, whiting, &c. *Best Months* : June to October. A chart of the Swanage and Bournemouth coast is given in Fig. 57.

Swansea (Glam.).—*Fishing* : Fair *Fish* : Bass, mullet, &c. *Best Months* : June to October

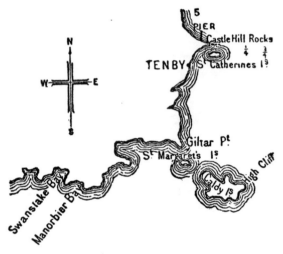

Fig. 78.—Chart of the Pembrokeshire Coast from Swanslake Bay to Tenby, showing the depth in fathoms. There are plenty of pollack and mackerel near Caldy Island.

Teignmouth (S. Devon).—*Fishing* : Good. *Fish* : Bass, dab, mackerel, plaice, pollack, whiting, &c. *Best Months* : July to September.

Tenby (Pemb.).—*Fishing* : Good. *Fish*: Bass, gurnard, mackerel, mullet, plaice, pollack, and whiting. *Best Months* : July to October. A chart of the coast from here to Swanslake Bay is given in Fig. 78.

Tintagel (Cornwall).—*Fishing* : Fair. *Fish*. Bass, pollack, gurnard, &c. *Best Months* : June to September.

Torcross (S. Devon).—*Fishing* : Good. *Fish* : Bass, bream, conger, flounders, gurnard, pollack, mackerel, &c. *Best Months* : September and October.

Torquay (S. Devon).—*Fishing* : Good. *Fish* : Bass, conger, crab, dab, lobster, mackerel, grey mullet, pollack, pout, smelt, whiting, &c. *Best Months* : May to October. A chart of Torbay is shown in Fig 79.

Totland Bay (I. of Wight).—*Fishing* : Good. *Fish* : Bass, conger, mackerel, whiting-pout. *Best Months* : May to November.

Traethsaith (Cardiganshire).—*Fishing* : Fair.

Trebarwith Strand (Cornwall).—*Fishing* : Fair. *Best Months* : June to October.

Tynemouth (Northumberland).—*Fishing* : Good. *Fish* : Cod, gurnard, mackerel, plaice, and whiting. *Best Months* : April to October.

Ventnor (I. of Wight).—*Fishing* : Fair. *Fish* : Bass, flounder, mackerel, pollack, rock-tench, whiting-pout, &c. *Best Months* : June to September. A chart of the Isle of Wight is given in Fig. 68.

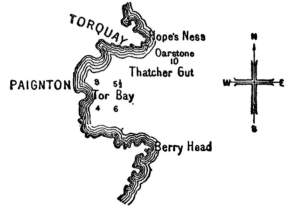

Fig. 79.—Chart of Torbay, showing the depth in fathoms. The bay is celebrated for dabs. Fine bass are taken off Paignton. Berry Head is a good spot for mackerel.

Walton-on-Naze (Essex).—*Fishing* : Fair. *Fish* : Codling, dab, eel, mullet, plaice, sole, whiting, &c. *Best Months* : June to October.

Warkworth (Northumberland).—*Fishing* : Good.

Watchet (Som.).—*Fishing* : Fair. *Fish* : Cod, conger, ling, and skate. *Best Months* : October to end of January.

Wells (Norfolk).—*Fishing* : Good. *Fish* : Brill, cod, mackerel, mullet, plaice, salmon-trout, &c. *Best Months* : March to October.

Westgate (Kent).—*Fishing* : Good. *Fish* : Bass, cod, mullet, &c. *Best Months* : July to October.

West Kirby (Cheshire).—*Fishing* : Poor.

West Lulworth (Dorset).—*Fishing* : Good. *Fish* : Bass, conger, pollack, whiting, &c. *Best Months* : August and September.

Weston-super-Mare (Som.).—*Fishing* : Fair. *Fish* : Cod, hake, ling, ray, whiting, &c. *Best Months* : September to March

Weymouth (Dorset).—*Fishing* : Very good.   *Fish* : Bass, bream, conger, dory, flat-fish, mackerel, mullet, pollack, rock-fish, whiting, wrasse, &c.   *Best Months* ; July to October.   A chart of Weymouth Bay and Portland is given in Fig. 80.

Whitby (Yorks.).—*Fishing* : Good   *Fish* : Coalfish, cod, gurnard, haddock mackerel, pollack, whiting, &c.   *Best Months* : August and September.

Whitley (Northumberland).—*Fishing* : Good.   *Fish* : Codling, gurnard haddock, whiting, &c.   *Best Months* ; June to November.

Whitstable (Kent).—*Fishing* : Good.   *Fish* ; Eel, oyster, plaice, skate, sole *Best Months* ; June to September.

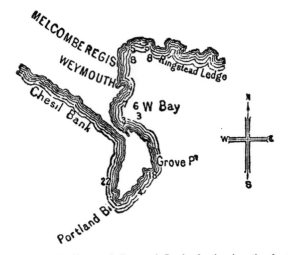

Fig. 80.—Chart of Weymouth Bay and Portland, showing the depth in fathoms. Weymouth is a capital station for ground-fish.

Withernsea (Yorks.).—*Fish* : Cod, whiting, flat-fish, and mackerel, &c.   *Best Months* : May onwards.

Worthing (Sussex).—*Fishing* : Fair.   *Fish* : Plaice, &c.   The coastline from here to Seaford is shown in the chart, Fig. 59, the crosses indicating the best grounds.

Yarmouth (Norfolk).—*Fishing* : Good.   *Fish* : Cod, codling, dab, mackerel, plaice, sea-trout, whiting, &c.   *Best Months* : July to November.

Yarmouth (I. of Wight).—*Fishing* : Good.   *Fish* : Bass, mackerel, mullet, pollack, pout, whiting, &c.   *Best Months* : May to December.

Yealmpton (S. Devon).—*Fishing* : Good.   *Fish* : Bass, pollack, &c.   *Best Months* : June to September.

Ynyslas (Cardiganshire).—*Fishing* : Fair.   *Fish* : Bass, mullet, &c

CHAPTER XIII

MOTOR-BOATS AND MOTORS FOR SEA FISHING

MOTIVE power is now being largely employed in connection with sea-fishing, and considerable improvements have been made in the various types of engines. It is intended to mention those chiefly suitable for amateurs who cannot afford the luxury of an expensive motor, and who do not require to seek very distant fishing-grounds. There are, doubtless, many of my readers who will continue to sail their own boats, and what more delightful or health-giving recreation can be found than moving swiftly over the waves in a good breeze, inhaling all the time the pure ozone? The effort of rowing provides splendid exercise, developing the heart and lungs, and can hardly be surpassed as a means of invigorating the system. One may often, however, wish to reach a remote fishing-ground, or the breeze may die away and prevent the boat from regaining the harbour. On such occasions "power" is of valuable assistance in enabling the amateur to pursue his sport with greater comfort and more profitable results.

One of the first successful outboard motors for fixing to the stern of rowing boats or dinghies was the Evinrude, an American make, and a wide range is now made from 2·2 to 54 h.p. Those who are accustomed to motor-cars will need reminding that the power of motor-boat engines is calculated on output at peak revolutions, not on the cylinder capacity. For small boats the Sport Single (2·2 h.p.) or the Lightwin (5·1 h.p.) are suitable. The smaller will propel a 12ft. dinghy at about 5 m.p.h., while the fuel tank holds enough for 1 to 1½ hours running. It weighs only 34lbs. Starting is by pulling on a cord. Both the exhaust and the carburettor intake are silenced. Further particulars of these and the larger models can be obtained from the London agent, Mr. George Spicer, Market Place, Brentford. Any Evinrude motor is available with reverse gear, and this is advised.

Another very good outboard engine for the angler is the Johnson Lightweight twin-cylinder 3-4 h.p., made in

America and marketed here by Vanadium Ltd., 64, Victoria Street, London, S.W. 1. The J.S.L. Bantam is an
all-British engine of $2\frac{1}{2}$ h.p., with forward and reverse gears,
which has also a neutral gear so that the engine can idle
with the boat stationary. The makers are Joseph Stubbs,
Ltd., Mill Street, Ancoats, Manchester. A still lighter
engine of British make is the 1·4 h.p. Turner-Bray (Arthur
Bray, Ltd., 114, Baker Street, London, W. 1). In spite of
its small size, this engine is claimed to propel a 12ft. dinghy
at 6 m.p.h.

When an outboard motor is used on a boat designed for
rowing, a certain amount of power is wasted. More speed,
or alternatively lower running costs, can be obtained with
a boat designed for power. A 12ft. motor dinghy with a
4 h.p. engine will accommodate four people and travel about
10 m.p.h. Running costs are about 10d. an hour. Boats
of this kind have been proved quite seaworthy. The lightest
engines, of about $2\frac{1}{2}$ h.p., will propel a well-laden dinghy in
fair conditions at 6 m.p.h.

Up to 30 or 40 h.p. the outboard motor has many advantages over the inboard (or built-in) motor. In small
sizes, about $2\frac{1}{2}$ h.p., it is portable, and can be carried on a
car and fitted on to a hired boat. It is usually cheaper
and often more efficient, costs nothing to install; being
very accessible and self-contained it is easier to maintain,
and it leaves the whole space of the boat for accommodation. Modern examples have a tilting device so that the
boat can be beached without trouble.

The types of inboard motor-boat are too numerous to
mention fully. Auxiliary yachts—*i.e.*, boats designed for
sailing but equipped with an engine—are very suitable for
sea fishing, as they combine the pleasure of sailing with
the ability to proceed to distant grounds or against contrary
winds and tides. Suitable lengths are from 25ft. to 32ft.
and ranging from 6 to 12 tons displacement. A good
example is the 7-ton model made by David Hillyard, Littlehampton. It is 28 ft. long and has sleeping accommodation
for two. The cabin cruiser is the corresponding class of
boat designed for power alone. It is to be had from about
20ft. to 50ft. in length, and those of 30ft. or more are

quite suitable for sea work. Such a boat can usually sleep
four, and with a 20 h.p. engine will travel at nearly
12 m.p.h.

For taking out fishing parties motor launches are very
useful. The accommodation is good and running costs are
low. The 15½ ft. launch of Brooke Marine Motors, Ltd.,
Lowestoft, can seat five easily, and its 5 h.p. engine propels
it at about 8 m.p.h. Larger types, 25ft. to 30ft. over all,
partly decked over for protection against spray, are very
well suited to sea fishing.

AEROPLANES. — Recent experiments with naval seaplanes in Southern California have shown that these
machines may be of great assistance in locating schools
of sardines, tuna, or other kinds of fish, and they might
also be of service on our coasts. When flying close to the
water, however, the vibration of the propeller would cause
fish swimming near the surface to become alarmed, and
they would descend immediately, thus defeating the object.
Even a seagull, when descending on a surface shoal, or
" shirmer," of pilchards, will cause them to disappear in a
moment. Seaplanes are now being used in America for
carrying parties of fishermen to suitable localities for sport,
and provide means for a novel kind of pastime exciting in
the highest degree.

As a final piece of advice, obtain a chart of the coast
you intend to visit, showing the depths of water and where
rocks are situated. Admiralty charts may be obtained
from Mr. J. D. Potter, 145, Minories, London, E. 1, the
catalogue being free on application.

INDEX.

Guide-book, 13
Gurnard, 28
  Skin as bait, 26
Gurnet, 28
Gut collars, tying, 10
  Fastenings for, 11
  for rod-fishing, 31
  Joining, 11
  Knots for, 11
  Steeping, 10
  Tying, 11
  Whipping, on to hooks, 12

H.

Haddock, 20
Hake, 28
Hand-lines, sizes of, 5
Hand-net fishing for shrimps, 68
Hermit-crab as bait, 17
Herring, 19
Hints, general, 72
Holder for hooks, 54
  for lines, 55
Hooking crabs, 62
Hooks, 10
  Attaching, 11
  Baiting, 15, 16
  Holder for, 54
  Kinds of, 10
  Launcing, 17
  Makers of, 10
  Sizes of, 10
  Swivel conger, 22
  Tying snood to, 12

J.

"Jack's" bag-net, 59
Jam knots, 12
January, fish in season in, 71
July, fish in season in, 71, 72
June, fish in season in, 71

K.

Killick, 73
  Bend, 49
Kinds of fish at various stations, 75

Kinking, prevention of, 5
Knife, bait, 15
Knots, fisherman's, 11
  Jam, 12
  Killick bend, 49
  Lark's-head, 40

L.

Lark's-head knot, 40
Last, 40
Launce or sand-eel, 16, 17, 34
Launcing-hook, 17
Leads, 7
  Improved, 34
  Sizes and shapes of, 7, 8
Lines, 2, 4, 5
  Barking, 6
  Bulters, 47
  Circus, 46
  Cod, 5
  Cotton, 5
  Deep-sea, 5, 47
  Dressing, 6
  Drift, 34
  Drying, 7
  Flax, 5
  for mackerel-railing, 39
  for night-fishing, 51
  for rocky-bottom fishing, 22 29
  for rod-fishing, 31
  for sandy-bottom fishing, 18-21
  Frames for, 6
  Hemp, 5
  Holder for, 55
  In-shore, 5
  Length of, 5
  Long, 46
  Ready for tackle, 8
  Rigging up, quickly, 8
  Stretching, 5
  Tanning, 6
  Traveller, 46
  Useful sizes of, 5
  Waterproofed, 5
  Weight of, 5
  Whalebone booms for, 8

Printed in Great Britain by
Billing and Sons Ltd., Guildford and Esher
F 6133